ŞEBNEM EROĞLU

POVERTY AND INTERNATIONAL MIGRATION

A Multi-Site and Intergenerational Perspective

POLICY PRESS SHORTS RESEARCH

First published in Great Britain in 2022 by

Policy Press, an imprint of
Bristol University Press
University of Bristol
1–9 Old Park Hill
Bristol
BS2 8BB
UK
t: +44 (0)117 374 6645
e: bup-info@bristol.ac.uk

Details of international sales and distribution partners are available at
policy.bristoluniversitypress.co.uk

British Library Cataloguing in Publication Data
A catalogue record for this book is available from the British Library

ISBN 978-1-4473-6573-0 hardcover
ISBN 978-1-4473-6574-7 ePub
ISBN 978-1-4473-6575-4 ePdf

Cover design: Bristol University Press
Front cover image: ullstein bild/contributor
Bristol University Press and Policy Press use environmentally responsible print partners.
Printed and bound in Great Britain by CPI Group (UK) Ltd, Croydon, CR0 4YY

FSC
www.fsc.org
MIX
Paper from responsible sources
FSC® C013604

Contents

List of figures and tables

Figure

Tables

Acknowledgements

The 2000 Families Survey database on which this book is based is an outcome of a five-year NORFACE-funded project (€2 million) performed in collaboration with teams based in Germany, the UK and the Netherlands under the leadership of Professor Ayşe Güveli (grant number: 235548). I am thankful to NORFACE (New Opportunities for Research Funding Agency Cooperation in Europe) for providing me with an opportunity to work with a wonderful team of researchers in bringing this ambitious research idea to life. I thank each and every member of the team not only for the immense effort they put into the creation of this unique dataset but also for making the research process an enjoyable one.

I am also grateful to my husband Jeremy and our delightful daughter, Ayla Iona, for being so understanding about the time I had to steal from them to complete this book.

Last but not least, I would like to express my gratitude to Professor Chris Pickvance FAcSS for the kind and generous support he has provided for me throughout my life in the UK. His faith in my academic abilities kept me going at times when I felt most rejected. I dedicate this book to him and my loving and caring grandmother, Makbule Baransel, both of whom have recently passed away.

ONE

Introduction

This is the first study to examine the poverty outcomes of international migration through comparisons of three family generations of 'settler' migrants spanning multiple destinations, with their returnee and stayer counterparts living in the country of origin. The study investigates group and generational differences in the extent and sources of monetary poverty, based on an adaptation of the resource-based model the author of this book developed originally to examine household responses to poverty (Eroğlu 2011, 2013). As well as tracing the generational trends, it examines and explains the degree of direct transmission on to younger generations of migrants and stayers. The research base for this book is the pioneering 2000 Families Survey, which a) locates male ancestors who moved from Turkey to Europe during the guest-worker years of 1964 to 1971 and their comparators who did not leave their origins, and b) charts their families in Turkey and Europe up to the fourth generation. The Survey led to the creation of the largest database on labour migration to Europe, currently deposited in GESIS (Ganzeboom et al 2016; Güveli et al 2016).

Drawing on this unique dataset, the book develops a multi-site and intergenerational viewpoint on migrant poverty with an aim to challenge the dominant thinking about international migration in terms of its (dis)benefits for the destination countries and join the growing efforts to bring the welfare and wellbeing of migrants and their descendants to the forefront of academic and policy agendas. Thereby, it makes a significant contribution to the underdeveloped parts of the international migration literature.

Within this literature, far less research attention has been paid to the poverty of migrants and their descendants beyond their incomes, earnings, wages, benefit claims and educational, employment and occupational status, despite the fact that poverty offers a better standpoint for welfare/wellbeing than any other indicator that accounts for labour market participation or state transfers only. An analysis of migrant poverty provides a vantage point on welfare particularly by a) allowing a focus on those at the bottom of the income distribution, b) encapsulating *all* individuals independently of their relationship with the labour market and c) capturing the collective contribution of education, employment/occupation and benefits transfers to individual or household welfare (Kazemipur and Halli 2001; Galloway and Aaberge 2005). Also, when measured at the household level, poverty as a concept potentially provides a better representation of the resources accessible to the individual and their welfare outcomes (Picot et al 2008).

Intriguingly, despite its discernible advantages, poverty of international migrants remains understudied. Moreover, as documented in Chapter Two, the existing literature hardly examines the relationship between poverty and international migration from a multi-site perspective. There is, in fact, a small but growing body of multi-site research that connects destination and origin countries through migrant–stayer comparisons, including the studies undertaken by the 2000 Families Project Team. The body of works published thus far from the 2000 Families Survey seeks to disentangle the impact of international migration on occupational and educational attainment, self-employment, asset accumulation, marriage patterns, intra-household decision making, religious beliefs, national identity, social relationships, gender attitudes and life satisfaction (Baykara-Krumme 2014, 2016, 2017; Güveli 2014; Spierings 2014; Güveli et al 2015; Baykara-Krumme and Platt 2018; Eroğlu 2018, 2020, 2021; Bayrakdar and Güveli 2021), but evidently, their focus does not extend to the underexplored relationship between poverty and international migration. In fact, none of the existing multi-site studies involve comparisons of poverty across multiple generations and destinations. The only poverty research from the *international* migration literature that compares migrants with stayers is performed by Sabates-Wheeler et al (2008), which links migrants to Italy with their origins but estimates poverty subjectively, based on people's self-evaluations of their predicament. There are two migrant–stayer comparisons that measure poverty objectively from a monetary perspective; however, these are studies from the *internal* migration literature, focussed on understanding the impact of the US Great Migration from the South to the North (Alexander et al 2017; Curtis 2018).

Besides, the international migration literature seldom examines the poverty status of the younger generation(s) as compared with the older generation(s). None of the existing works are based on nested family design; they rarely use matched (that is, dyadic) parent–child information to link generations, and in rare cases where such a family link is established, the focus remains restricted to child poverty (Oropesa and Landale 1997; Van Hook et al 2004; Thomas 2011). Hence, until now, important questions about intergenerational transmission of migrant poverty have remained unexplored.

The existing literature predominantly approaches the relationship between poverty and international migration from an origin- or destination-based perspective (see Chapter Two for a full list of relevant citations). The origin-based studies examine the role of poverty in driving international migration or the poverty consequences of this process with a particular focus on the contribution of migrant remittances to the wealth or welfare of the left-behind populations. The destination-based research is, on the other hand, fundamentally interested in testing out the assimilationist expectations of a positive change in migrants' predicaments over time and across generations, largely drawing on comparisons between migrants and 'natives'. The migrant–native comparisons, however, only tell us about one side of the story. To paint a fuller picture of the economic (dis)benefits of migration, one also needs to answer the counterfactual question – that is, what would have happened should they have not left their origins? While it remains impossible to fully establish the outcomes of unmade choices in the social world, this book successfully approximates the counterfactual through unparalleled migrant–stayer comparisons of monetary poverty and its transmission across family generations spanning Turkey and Europe.

Overall, the book makes a unique contribution to the international migration literature through the three major innovations it brings to the study of migrant poverty. Firstly, by taking a *multi-site approach* that allows the settler and return migrants to be compared with their stayer counterparts who did not leave their origins, it provides a rare insight into the economic (dis)benefits of international migration and the counterfactual question. Secondly, based on a *nested survey design* that charts family members of migrants and stayers up to the fourth generation, the book takes an unparalleled *intergenerational perspective* that allows an exploration of the generational trends in migrant poverty as well as its *direct* transmission from parents to their *own* children. Finally, unlike most quantitative studies on the topic, the book takes a *theory-driven approach* to understanding the root causes of migrant poverty by adapting the resource-based framework developed previously by the author (Eroğlu 2011, 2013) to the international migration context, and using it to inform the statistical models estimated. The new model represents the most comprehensive portrayal provided to date of the micro- and macro-level influences upon migrant poverty and their interactions with migrants' resources and economic actions. By placing international migration within the broader framework of household resources and livelihoods, it also establishes the theoretical link claimed to be missing from existing conceptualisations of the migration-development nexus (De Haas 2010).

The structure of this book is organised as follows. Chapter Two provides an overview of the previous findings about the incidence, persistence and sources of migrant poverty while positioning this body of research within the wider literature exploring the relationships between international migration, poverty and other welfare and performance indicators. Following a review of relevant concepts, theories and measurement methods, Chapter Three introduces the approach taken in this study to define and measure migrant poverty and explain its sources. Chapter Four outlines the key features of the target population and the sample, along with the research design and methods used for sampling, data collection and analysis. Chapter Five presents the results obtained from descriptive and multi-variable (probit) analyses of the Survey data as well as narrating the story behind. Chapter Six concludes with a discussion of their implications for theory, research and policy.

TWO

Migrant poverty: scoping the empirical field

This chapter maps out the empirical works focussed on the relationship between poverty and international migration while situating them within the wider literature that qualitatively or quantitatively examines the socio-economic performances of international migrants and/or their descendants. It then presents the current research evidence on the incidence, persistence and determinants of migrant poverty. It concludes by explaining the ways in which this book will contribute to closing the gaps existing within the field.

Situating migrant poverty research

There has been a long-standing research interest in understanding the socio-economic outcomes of international migration for the migrants and/or their descendants. Much of the literature is destination-oriented and targeted at different migrant groups or generations living in Europe, North America and other economically advanced parts of the world, including those with origins in Turkey. The outcomes are examined quantitatively and/or qualitatively, based on a wide range of performance indicators, but most are couched in terms of income or social mobility. Typically used measures include the wages, incomes, earnings and, more specifically, welfare transfers on one side (for example, Chiswick 1978; Blau 1984; Tienda and Jensen 1986; Borjas 1987; Borjas and Hilton 1996; Hammarstedt 2001; Aguilera and Massey 2003; Büchel and Frick 2005; Brown 2007; Reitz et al 2011; Stillman et al 2015; Gibson et al 2018; Villarreal and Tamborini 2018; Lightman and Gingrich 2018; Lamb et al 2021), and education, (un)employment and occupational attainment on the other (for example, Boyd 1984; Crul and Vermeulen 2003; Van Tubergen et al 2004; Kogan 2006; Van Tubergen 2006; Kasinitz et al 2008; Levels and Dronkers 2008; Fleischmann and Dronkers 2010; Luthra and Waldinger 2010; Kalter 2011; Pichler 2011; Crul et al 2012; Dustmann et al 2012; Lessard-Phillips et al 2012; Louie 2012; Ichou 2014; Spörlein and Van Tubergen 2014; Zuccotti et al 2017; Eroğlu 2018; Bayrakdar and Güveli 2021).

The above-sketched literature largely reflects the international migration scholars' general preoccupation with questions around assimilation, integration, incorporation or adaptation into the destination context, given the predominant use of the 'natives' as the comparator group to assess the socio-economic performances of migrants and/or their descendants. Migrant–native comparisons are, however, considered to provide a poor estimate of the counterfactual due to potential migrant selectivity. Migrants are regarded as a self-selected group with observed or unobserved characteristics that systematically distinguish them from those who do not migrate (Chiswick 1986). To fully separate the self-selection effect from that of migration, people's pre- and post-migration status would have to be compared. The social world, however, rarely presents researchers with an opportunity to draw such comparisons. The works of Stillman et al (2015) and Gibson et al (2018), which examine the migration impact on income, comprise the only two studies that were able to exploit this opportunity. Given the impracticality of a longitudinal or an experimental design within the context of international migration, migrant–stayer (multi-site) comparisons are drawn instead to approximate the counterfactual in the best way possible. However, those exploring the socio-economic outcomes for migrants still remain in the minority (Ichou 2014; Güveli et al 2015; Stillman et al 2015; Zuccotti et al 2017; Gibson et al 2018; Bayrakdar and Güveli 2021; Eroğlu 2021). These multi-site studies provide a rare insight into the economic (dis)benefits of international migration for the bearers of the process by shifting the emphasis more towards understanding the nature and extent of 'dissimilation' from migrant origins. Transcending the 'methodological nationalism' that is claimed to permeate the international migration literature (Amelina and Faist 2012), they further cross-border research in the field, which rarely spans 'non-Western' destinations, or explicitly links migrant origins to destinations.[1]

The socio-economic performances of migrants and their descendants are also examined from a generational viewpoint, based on a single cohort or multiple cohorts. Much of the relevant research draws on migrant cohorts, determined by looking at the person's country of birth and age on arrival in the destination country. Among the studies of migrant cohorts, the first and/or second generation are studied more widely (for example, Portes and Rumbaudt 2001; Crul and Vermeulen 2003; Kasinitz et al 2008; Levels and Dronkers 2008; Crul et al 2012; Dustmann et al 2012; Lessard-Phillips et al 2012; Louie 2012; Zuccotti et al 2017) than the third generation (see, for example, Brown 2007; Crul et al 2019). Indeed, few studies focus on the *family* generations to trace generational trends and/or to explore the role of intergenerational transfers (Telles and Ortiz 2008; Ichou 2014; Güveli et al 2015; Eroğlu 2018, 2021; Bayrakdar and Güveli 2021).

1 For further exceptions, see, for example, the works of Van Tubergen et al (2004), Fleischmann and Dronkers (2010) and Spörlein and Van Tubergen (2014).

A substantial part of the literature presented above documents the (comparative) disadvantages of migrants and/or their descendants and examines their sources. There are, however, deviations from this general tendency, which rather speak of a 'second-generation advantage' (Alba et al 2011: 770). Increasing attention is now being paid to the successful descendants of migrants and the newly emerging elite among this group (for example, Kasinitz et al 2008; Louie 2012; Crul et al 2017; Keskiner and Crul 2017; Konyalı 2017; Rezai 2017). These studies examine the costs and rewards of their success along with its determinants using the aforementioned language and indicators of social mobility. Other manifestations of migrant success and failure, however, remain understudied: asset and wealth attainment is one (for recent works see, for example, Lightman and Gingrich 2018; Keister et al 2020; Salgado and Ortiz 2020; Eroğlu 2021), and poverty is another. A detailed review of the existing research on migrant assets and wealth can be found in Eroğlu (2021).

In the remainder of this chapter, the focus will be on works that empirically explore the poverty status of the international migrants and their descendants who are still living in destination countries or have returned to their origins. For sake of brevity, this part of the literature will be referred to as migrant poverty research, recognising that the native-born descendants of migrants may not be called 'migrants' in the strict sense of the term. Migrant poverty literature is separate from the two major streams of research performed mostly within the development studies field to examine the relationship between poverty and international migration merely from an origin-based perspective. One of these streams examines the drivers of migratory decisions and flows, with a particular emphasis on the role played by poverty, income or wealth status of the potential and actual migrants (for example, Stark and Taylor 1989; Abramitzky et al 2013, Bertoli et al 2013; Hatlebakk 2016; Cojanu and Stroe 2017). The other investigates the poverty outcomes of international migration for the left-behind populations at the household, local community and/or country levels, often through a focus on the remittances (for example, Murrugarra et al 2011; Gibson et al 2013; Margolis et al 2013; Mohanty et al 2016; Vacaflores 2018; Wagle and Devkota 2018; Imran et al 2020). Neither of these streams is of direct relevance to the main quest of this book because even though the left-behind populations embrace migrants' stayer counterparts, the primary concern here is to understand the poverty impact of international migration on the movers themselves, not the left-behind.

Despite the long history of research on the socio-economic impact of international migration, and the central importance of poverty as an indicator of human welfare or wellbeing, until the early 2000s little interest has been taken in the subject of migrant poverty. Since then, there has been an increase in the number of poverty studies targeted at international migrants to economically advanced parts of the world. Among these, only the work of Sabates-Wheeler et al (2008) explicitly links a single migrant destination to multiple origins to assess poverty subjectively among the international migrants to Italy, as compared with their stayer counterparts in Ghana and Egypt. There is also little research dedicated specifically to understanding the poverty status of international migrants who returned to their origins (for example, Sabates-Wheeler et al 2007; Pratomo and Jayanthahumaran 2018).

The bulk of the existing migrant poverty research is oriented towards migrant destinations, and mostly involves single-country case studies, spanning Canada (Kazemipur and Halli 2001; Fleury 2007; Picot et al 2008), Denmark (Jakobsen and Pedersen 2017), Germany (Heizmann and Böhnke 2016), Italy (Berti et al 2014; Arcagni et al 2019), Luxembourg (Pi Alperin 2008), Norway (Galloway and Aaberge 2005), Spain (Muñozoz de Bustillo and Anton 2011; Carpio 2017), Sweden (Hammarstedt 2001; Hansen and Wahlberg 2009; Obucina 2014) and the United States (Jensen 1991; Oropesa and Landale 1997; Chapman and Bernstein 2003; Van Hook et al 2004;

Sullivan and Ziegert 2008; Thomas 2011; Emeka 2016; Young et al 2018). The cross-country comparisons performed are largely based within Europe, covering between two and 30 migrant destinations (Blume et al 2007; Lelkes 2007; Lelkes and Zólyomi 2011; Corrigan 2014; Hooijer and Picot 2015; Kesler 2015; Bárcena-Martìn and Pérez-Moreno 2017). Only the country coverage of Eugster's (2018) research extends beyond Europe.

The great majority of these studies conceive of migrant poverty in terms of earning below an objectively defined minimum (see Chapter Three for a detailed review of the measurement methods used). They typically investigate adult or household poverty among migrant populations at working age or older. Those with a focus on specific population groups, such as migrants' own children (for example, Oropesa and Landale 1997; Van Hook et al 2004; Galloway et al 2009; Thomas 2011; Gustafsson and Österberg 2018) or elderly migrants (Jakobsen and Pedersen 2017) are fewer in number.

Migrant versus 'native' comparisons also predominate this part of the literature. Within-migrant analyses indeed remain a rarity (Picot et al 2008; Sullivan and Ziegert 2008; Eugster 2018; Arcagni et al 2019). There is one study that combines the 'natives' and earlier migrants to compare with recent migrants (Fleury 2007).

Migrant poverty studies with a generational focus are more limited in number. Some of these specifically investigate the poverty of migrants' children aged below 18 years, covering one to three generations (Oropesa and Landale 1997; Van Hook et al 2004; Thomas 2011; Gustafsson and Österberg 2018). However, the first, second and third generations referred to in these studies represent migrant cohorts, identified using information about the birthplace of the children and their parents. They correspond to the foreign-born children, the native-born children with foreign-born parent(s) and the native-born children with native parent(s), respectively. The existing works on adult poverty of migrants and/or their descendants span a maximum of two generations that are also characterised by migrant cohorts (Kazemipur and Halli 2001; Emeka 2016; Heizmann and Böhnke 2016). For example, the latter two treat those who moved before and after a certain age (6 or 10 respectively) as the first and the second generation. Within the migration literature, this group of migrants are sometimes referred to as the 1.5 generation. Overall, current generational studies rarely establish the family link between cohorts, and then only to investigate child poverty (Oropesa and Landale 1997; Van Hook et al 2004; Thomas 2011). They seldom explore change in the predicaments of the younger generation(s) relative to older generation(s) and lack a focus on the intergenerational transmission of poverty.

Clearly, there exist no studies of multiple family generations that compare international migrants' objective poverty status with that of their stayer counterparts, including the returnees as the third comparator. Having mapped out the field, let us now summarise the emerging evidence on the extent and sources of migrant poverty.

Incidence and persistence of migrant poverty

The migrant–native comparisons performed to date unequivocally confirm that migrants are more disadvantaged across *all* destination contexts studied. However, except for those cases where migrants are treated as an aggregate group (Kazemipur and Halli 2001; Muñozoz de Bustillo and Anton 2011), substantial variation is shown to exist across migrant groups and destinations. Destination-oriented studies divide migrants into various sub-groups, for example, based on their origins (using information about the country, region or continent they come from and its EU membership status or level of economic development), sub-regions of the country they moved to, migration history (for instance, recent versus earlier migrants), legal standing (for instance, citizenship or refugee status) or 'racial'/ethnic identity. In the following, the observed variations between migrants to European destinations will be summarised.

Of the comparative studies spanning 14 to 30 EU countries, some document increased risk of poverty for migrants living in 'non-mixed' households with no native-born members (Bárcena-Martìn and Pérez-Moreno 2017). Others indicate the risk to be greater for the non-EU migrants than the EU-born (Lelkes 2007; Lelkes and Zólyomi 2011; Corrigan 2014). The same pattern emerges from the single-country case studies of migrant poverty in Spain and Luxembourg (Pi Alperin 2008; Carpio 2017) and of the low-income distribution in Sweden (Hammarstedt 2001). For example, Pi Alperin (2008) suggests that foreigners born outside the EU15 are particularly impoverished. Similarly, Hammarstedt (2001) demonstrates the probability of having a low disposable income to be greater among non-EU migrants. He finds that the share of individuals with a low disposable income is the highest for migrants from Asia. Likewise, Galloway and Aaberge (2005) locate those coming from Asian countries (including Turkey) among the top three most impoverished migrant groups in Norway.

The research that clusters migrants according to the economic development level of their country of origin produces similar results. For example, Blume et al (2007) documents those who moved to Denmark and Sweden from the less developed parts of the world to be significantly more impoverished. The risk of poverty is reported to be greater in Denmark. Relative to Danes, who hardly experience poverty in old age, the elderly migrants (aged 60–74) with origins in Turkey, Iraq, Pakistan and Vietnam are shown to experience considerably higher levels of poverty (Jakobsen and Pedersen 2017). Those from Turkey aged 65 or above exhibit the highest rates. Other single case studies from Germany and Sweden also place migrants with origins in Turkey among the most disadvantaged in terms of the incidence and persistence of poverty (Hansen and Wahlberg 2009; Obucina 2014; Heizmann and Böhnke 2016).

This group of migrants is shown to suffer more intense poverty in Sweden than in Germany (Kesler 2015).

Overall, there is consistent evidence to establish that migrants are more impoverished than 'natives'. The proponents of the assimilation theory expect that as time passes and they become more familiar with the destination context within which they operate, their economic performance or wellbeing will improve, or converge with those of the 'natives' (for example, Alba and Nee 1997). They recognise the adjustment challenges faced by the migrants and the sacrifices they make to become established within the new environment, but consider these to be short-lived (for example, Todaro 1969), and anticipate the prospects for the subsequent generations to be even more favourable. Others, however, draw attention to various structural factors that can lead to segmented (for example, downward) assimilation of migrants and their descendants (Gans 1992; Portes and Zhou 1993). Let us now review the cross-sectional, longitudinal and generational research evidence to ascertain the degree to which the assumptions of the assimilation theory have been confirmed within the specific case of migrant poverty.

A central question here concerns the extent to which the poverty status of international migrants has improved over time. The destination-based studies approach this question in different ways. The group of studies that look at years elapsed since migration (YSM) reveals its complex relationship with poverty. Blume et al's (2007) longitudinal study of migrants to Denmark and Sweden records a decline in poverty rates with increased YSM. The same relationship is also observed among migrants to Norway; yet it appears inapplicable to those coming from Asian countries such as Turkey. Moreover, the case studies of Canada, Germany and the US demonstrate the poverty-reducing effect of YSM to be very small (Kazemipur and Halli 2001; Sullivan and Zeigert 2008; Heizmann and Böhnke 2016). The comparative research by Kesler (2015) on migrants to Germany, Sweden and the UK shows that while men's YSM makes a positive difference, a large poverty gap remains even between long-term migrants and 'natives' (Kesler 2015). Obucina's (2014) longitudinal study of migrants to Sweden reports a greater tendency for migrants with increased YSM to exit poverty, which is, however, attributed to cohort differences rather than the time elapsed since arrival. Research by Jakobsen and Perdersen (2017) suggests that the poverty risk for elderly migrants to Denmark reduces only *after 20 years* in the country. Finally, Arcagni et al (2019) find no significant relationship between multi-dimensional poverty and the time spent in the destination by migrants to Italy.

Studies based on descriptive trend analyses also provide little evidence of improvement over time. While the work of Chapman and Bernstein (2003) documents a more rapid decline in the poverty rates for earlier and later migrants to the US than the 'natives' over the period between 1994 and 2000, the rates remain well above those for the 'natives'. In their comparative study of migrants to 25 European countries, Lelkes and Zólyomi (2011) report no major change between 2004 and 2007 in the poverty rates, especially for those born outside Europe. Heizmann and Böhnke (2016) show that over the period between 1991 and 2011, rates increased much more rapidly for migrants with more than 18 YSM, converging with the rates for migrants who spent 18 or fewer years in Germany. A case study of Spain by Muñozoz de Bustillo and Anton (2011) reveals that the incidence, intensity and severity of both moderate and extreme poverty are not only greater for the migrants than the 'natives' but that they are also remarkably constant over the 2003–2007 period. Carpio (2017) complements these findings by demonstrating a more rapid increase in the poverty levels of migrants following the financial crisis of 2008.

The longitudinal evidence obtained from more dynamic analyses of migrant poverty also suggests marginal improvement. A within-group analysis of migrants who moved to Canada in the past 12 years shows that while the probability of falling into poverty declines for this group of migrants after the first year of their arrival, they remain highly likely to experience chronic poverty over a ten-year period (Picot et al 2008). Migrant–native comparisons yield complementary results. A case study of Sweden by Hansen and Wahlberg (2009) spanning the 1991–2001 period confirms the probability of entering poverty to be significantly greater for the migrants who also exhibit lower exit probabilities. These findings are supported and complemented by further research on Sweden, which demonstrates the chances of 'leaving poverty and staying out of it' to be significantly lower for migrants than 'natives' (Obucina 2014: 19).

So, how does the generational evidence on migrant poverty contribute to this picture? Despite the varied nature of the populations and the cohorts covered, the emerging results converge in their limited support for the assimilationist viewpoint, which predicts even brighter prospects for the descendants of migrants. Of the existing works that specifically focus on migrants' children aged 17 or below, the Swedish case study by Galloway et al (2009) shows that while child poverty declines with increased parental duration of stay, the children of migrants – especially those with parental origins in low- to middle-income countries – experience poverty to a much higher extent than the 'natives', even if their parents had long-term residency. These findings are supported by further research on Sweden, which documents increased poverty among the children of migrants (including the second generation) as 'natives' poverty declines (Gustafsson and Österberg 2018). Case studies from the US provide further evidence, confirming the racially conditioned nature of poverty among migrants' children (Oropesa and Landale 1997; Van Hook et al 2004; Thomas 2011). For example, research by Thomas (2011) demonstrates the diminished returns from increased parental education among black migrant children.

The generational studies targeted at adult populations paint a similar picture. The descriptive analysis by Heizmann and Böhnke

(2016) indicates lower poverty rates for the second generation of migrants to Germany as compared with their first-generation counterparts; however, between the years of 1991 and 2011, the poverty rates for the second generation remain consistently above those for the 'natives'. A US case study by Emeka (2016) points to the gendered and racially differentiated nature of the poverty outcomes for the first- and second-generation migrants by demonstrating the pronounced disadvantages experienced by Black Africans as compared with white South Africans and the native-born whites, regardless of their generational status. Similarly, Kazemipur and Halli's (2001) research on Canada records higher poverty rates among the second generation of migrants than their first-generation counterparts.

Taken together, the cross-sectional, longitudinal and generational research evidence lends little support to the assimilationist assumptions about the socio-economic performance and wellbeing of migrants and their descendants. They tend to be poorer than the 'natives' while the extent of their impoverishment varies across migrant groups and destinations. The picture appears to be particularly bleak for the non-whites and the migrants who originated from economically less developed parts of the world. But does this mean that the migration journey was not economically worthwhile? Would the migrants and their descendants have been less impoverished had they stayed in the origin country? These questions cannot be fully answered through migrant–native comparisons, on which much of the migrant poverty research is based. It is, however, clear from the evidence that their impoverishment persists over time and across generations while exhibiting little convergence with that of the 'natives'. In this respect, their migration journey cannot be said to have been very successful. A firmer judgement about the migration effect would require comparing pre- and post-migration levels of poverty; however, longitudinal studies of this nature are non-existent within this part of the literature. There are three migrant–stayer comparisons performed to approximate the counterfactual, but two of these are from the field of *internal* migration (Alexander et al 2017; Curtis 2018). Nonetheless, the evidence obtained from these three pieces of research will be reviewed next to shed further light upon the poverty impact of migration.

The conventional view expects migrants to fare better economically than the stayers after some initial challenges to adjustment (for example, Lee 1966; see also Eichenlaub et al 2010 and Curtis 2018 for an extended review). Congruent with this expectation are the findings of Sabates-Wheeler et al (2008), indicating that Ghanaian and Egyptian migrants to Italy are subjectively less impoverished than their counterparts who stayed in Egypt and Ghana. This study measures subjective poverty using information about the views of migrants and stayers regarding the sufficiency of their current and past (that is, pre-migration in the case of the former) income to meet basic needs. The credibility of these findings may be questioned considering the absence of clarity and consistency around what basic needs entail.

The other two studies, which objectively assess the poverty outcomes of the US Great Migration from the South to the North, are less supportive of the conventional wisdom. Of these, the work of Alexander et al (2017) reports only a marginal improvement in the second-generation migrants' probability of falling into poverty as compared with Southern stayers. Extending the migrant–stayer comparisons to include the returnees, Curtis's (2018) research highlights the diverse and conflicting consequences of migration in terms of reducing racial differentials in poverty.

Regarding the poverty status of international migrants who returned to their origins, very little remains known empirically. According to one dominant view, the return migrants are less favourably selected than those migrants who stayed on in the destination country in terms of observed and unobserved skills and traits that help one thrive in receiving societies and economies (Chiswick 1986). This view construes the returnees as failed migrants; therefore, its logical extension would be to expect greater poverty among them. The sparse evidence existing within the field lends little support to this view. A recent cross-sectional study of international migrants who returned to their origin country confirms their reduced likelihood of falling into poverty but predicts them not to stay out of poverty for long due to their inability to make productive use of their financial capital accumulations (Pratomo and Jayanthakumaran 2018). While the wider international migration literature provides some support for this prediction, for example, by demonstrating an increased propensity for the return migrants to waste skills and remain economically inactive (Coniglio and Brzozowski 2018), it produces more evidence to counter it. Some studies find increased entrepreneurial activity among the returnees with greater savings (McCormick and Wahba 2001; Piracha and Vadean 2010). Others report the benefits of international migration for their asset or wealth accumulations. Specifically, Wong and his colleagues (2007) detect a long-term positive effect on personal wealth from migration for middle- or old-age returnees from the United States to Mexico. More recently, Eroğlu (2021) compares the non-financial investments made in the current country of residence by three family generations of migrants from Turkey to Europe with their stayer counterparts to find that across all generations, the propensity for such investments is the greatest for the returnees and lowest for those continuing to live in Europe.

To conclude, this section reviewed the findings about the extent of migrant poverty emerging from the destination-based research as well as the rare studies performed from a multi-site perspective or from the origin-based viewpoint of return migration. Whichever angle is taken, the weight of evidence contradicts the assimilationist expectation that as time goes by, migrants and their descendants based in destination contexts will fare as well as the 'natives' and outperform the stayers and the returnees.

Determinants of migrant poverty

This section will review the individual-, household- and country-level forces that are empirically demonstrated to bear a significant relationship with migrant poverty.

Starting with the individual-level factors, age and gender are rarely given centre stage within migrant poverty research. Migrants are shown to be more exposed to the risk of poverty in old age than their native counterparts (Jakobsen and Pedersen 2017), while being young is found not to increase the risk significantly (Bárcena-Martìn and Pérez-Moreno 2017). As for gender, female second-generation migrants from Africa to the US are reported to experience greater improvement in their poverty status as compared with their male counterparts (Emeka 2016).

The research attention is directed more towards understanding the role of 'race', ethnicity and migration origins, history and status. Within this part of the literature, the categories of 'race', ethnicity and migrant origins are typically treated as individual attributes and rarely articulated as an institutional, contextual or structural factor to draw attention to the poverty-inducing effects of systemic racism, or public hostility directed at migrants and their descendants and the discriminatory practices that stem from it (for an exception see, for example, Obucina 2014). Although some within-migrant analyses detect no 'race' effect (Sullivan and Ziegert 2008), the systematic evidence presented earlier consistently shows that the most disadvantaged are the non-whites and migrants who originated from economically less developed parts of the world (Hammerstedt 2001; Galloway and Aaberge 2005; Blume et al 2007; Hansen and Wahlberg 2009; Lelkes and Zólyomi 2011; Corrigan 2014; Obucina 2014; Emeka 2016; Heizmann and Böhnke 2016; Jakobsen and Pedersen 2017).

The poverty implications of one's migration history are investigated mostly through a focus on age at migration and/or YSM (interchangeably referred to as duration of stay). As documented earlier, there is considerable consensus upon the limited effect of time spent abroad in reducing migrant poverty (Kazemipur and Halli 2001; Sullivan and Ziegert 2008; Kesler, 2015; Heizmann and Böhnke 2016; Arcagni et al 2019). The evidence regarding the impact of age at migration is, however, more mixed. Elder people who migrated at a young age are shown to experience poverty in contexts where it ceases to pose a problem for the 'natives' (Jakobsen and Pedersen 2017). However, the risk is found to be significantly greater for migrants who arrived at a later stage of their life course (Kazemipur and Halli 2001).

Migration status is studied more in terms of citizenship and refugee status to understand the poverty impact of migrants' legal standing. Significant disparities in poverty are detected, for example, among the native-born and naturalised citizens and the non-citizens (Young et al 2018). The non-citizens and the refugees are documented to be at greater risk of poverty than other migrant groups (for example, Sullivan and Ziegert 2008; Hansen and Wahlberg 2009). Those migrants who were able to travel with formal documents are found more likely to have moved out of poverty by the time of their return to their origins (Sabates-Wheeler et al 2007).

The educational and social resources possessed by migrants, their descendants and/or their parents are also examined. The impact of the former is explored through a particular focus on years of schooling or highest qualifications achieved. Increased poverty is often associated with the low educational attainment of migrants or their parents, and *vice versa* (for example, Kazemipur and Halli 2001; Van Hook et al 2004; Sullivan and Ziegert 2008). However, growing attention is now being paid to the poverty-inducing effect of diminishing returns obtained from (parental) education (Fleury 2007; Picot et al 2008; Emeka 2016; Bárcena-Martìn and Pérez-Moreno 2017). As for social resources, their role is examined from the viewpoint of social capital to demonstrate the significance of intra- and inter-ethnic ties in alleviating migrant poverty (Heizmann and Böhnke 2016).

At the household level, the focus has been on understanding the influence of factors such as household size and membership composition. Households with more (dependent) children are found to be more impoverished (Sullivan and Ziegert 2008; Bárcena-Martìn and Pérez-Moreno 2017). The absence of native-born members in the family is also shown to significantly increase the poverty risk (Bárcena-Martìn and Pérez-Moreno 2017).

While most research is geared towards understanding the possible effects of individual- and household-level factors, recent multi-level analyses of migrant poverty show that much of the observed variation is attributable to influences operating at the country level (Corrigan 2014; Bárcena-Martìn and Pérez-Moreno 2017). The likely influences explored at this level relate to labour market forces and the immigration and welfare policies of receiving country governments.

Labour market-related effects are often examined indirectly from the viewpoint of employment. Poverty is linked here to part-time work (Kazemipur and Halli 2001) and lower parental employment status (Van Hook et al 2004). More recently, however, employment is shown to have a limited impact in terms of reducing the probability of falling into poverty for migrants, as compared with the 'natives' (Bárcena-Martìn and Pérez-Moreno 2017). The relative disadvantages of poor migrants are attributed to a) their possession of lower levels of country-specific (for example, language) skills, b) undervaluation of the educational skills and qualifications they have acquired abroad and c) discrimination in the labour market (Obucina 2014).

Regarding welfare-related effects, earlier studies highlight the significance of participation in social security and active labour market programmes for migrant poverty within a single-country context (for example, Galloway and Aaberge 2005). More recent cross-country and inter-state studies draw attention to migrant participation in the labour market and welfare programmes, their interactions with the receiving governments' immigration policies and the conditionality attached to their citizenship or residency status. They document increased poverty for migrants living in countries or states that constrain their access to work and welfare with their less 'inclusive' or more conditional immigration policies (Blume et al 2007; Corrigan 2014; Kesler 2015; Bárcena-Martìn and Pérez-Moreno 2017; Eugster 2018; Young et al 2018). The extent of labour market (de)regulation and welfare generosity is also shown to matter (Corrigan 2014; Hooijer and Picot 2015; Eugster 2018). For example, the combination of high conditionality with low levels of welfare generosity is suggested to lead to the highest levels of poverty among third-country nationals (Corrigan 2014). Likewise, the poverty-reducing effects of more regulated labour markets and generous welfare programmes are found to be stronger in contexts where migrants are granted easier access to paid work and welfare benefits (Eugster 2018). Further evidence shows that it is the 'unwanted' migrants from outside the EU27 who are denied the full benefits of generous welfare states (Hooijer and Picot 2015).

While the existing research literature unearths a range of important factors spanning the individual, household and country levels, most of the explanations provided for migrant poverty remain data driven. Some theorising around its determinants does exist, but existing theories focus either on a specific factor, such as social capital (Heizmann and Böhnke 2016), or a sub-group of factors to make sense of the relationships between a) work, conditionality, legal status and welfare (Corrigan 2014; Eugster 2018; Young et al 2018), or b) assimilation (that is, migration year and age), human capital (that is, years of schooling) and the wider structure (that is, employment type and sector) (Kazemipur and Halli 2001). Evidently, the current literature is bereft of a comprehensive framework that conceptualises the notion of migrant poverty and its key determinants.

Conclusion

This chapter sought to map the contours of the wider literature exploring the socio-economic performance of migrants and/or their descendants. It situated the existing works on migrant poverty as a body of research that is separate from origin-based studies that examine the role of poverty in driving international migration or its poverty consequences for the left-behind populations.

The review of these works demonstrated the convergence of evidence indicating increased poverty for migrants as compared with 'natives' and its persistence over time and across generations. The non-white and non-EU migrants with origins in economically less developed countries were shown to be particularly disadvantaged. Multiple explanations were provided for their impoverishment, spanning the individual, household and country levels. The contextual influences linked with the labour market and government policy concerning, for example, the areas of employment, welfare and immigration were suggested to play a particularly significant role in shaping migrant poverty.

The review also highlighted two distinct gaps existing within the field: one is more empirical in nature and concerns the lack of multi-site and intergenerational research to answer the counterfactual question and to explore the nature and extent of transmission across family generations. The other has to do with the absence of an all-encompassing framework that demarcates the boundaries of migrant poverty as a concept and theorises about its multiple sources and their interplays with the processes of international migration. This book will bridge both gaps, starting with the theoretical one.

THREE

Theorising and measuring migrant poverty

Unlike much of the existing research on the subject, this study adopts a theory-driven approach to investigating migrant poverty. This chapter thus aims to define the concept and explain why the methods chosen to measure it had to diverge from the ideal. It starts by evaluating the main approaches used previously to define and measure poverty and then presents the approach taken here. Following a critical evaluation of relevant theories from the wider international migration literature, it introduces the core components of the resource-based model adapted from the author's earlier work (Eroğlu 2011, 2013) to examine the relationships between poverty and international migration. The chapter concludes by setting out research hypotheses for statistical testing.

Defining and measuring (migrant) poverty

Throughout its long history, the concept of poverty has come to be defined and measured in many different ways. There has been an extensive academic debate around the question of whether poverty should be understood in absolute or relative terms.

The absolutists conceive of poverty as having an 'irreducible' core that is independent of context (Sen 1983: 159). Sen, for example, persuasively argues for maintaining the notion of 'absolute need' to be able to distinguish poverty from wider inequalities. This viewpoint is evident not only within the earlier subsistence (Booth 1891; Rowntree 1910) and basic needs approaches to poverty (ILO 1976; Streeton et al 1981), but also within the more contemporary works developed from the capability perspective (for example, Sen 1993, 1999; Alkire and Santos 2014; Anand et al 2020).

The relativists reject the absolute understanding of poverty by arguing that the requirements of life vary across time and space; therefore, people in need or poverty should be defined by looking at other people living in the same society at the same time. One of the most well-known representatives of this perspective is the relative deprivation approach pioneered by Townsend (1979), who conceptualises poverty as being deprived of the living standards widely approved and shared within a given society. Most prominent variants of this approach redefine the concept as 'the enforced lack of socially perceived necessities' (for example, Mack and Lansley 1985 Halleröd 1994; Gordon et al 2000). The relativists consider the absolute versus relative poverty distinction to be untenable given the use of context-specific indicators even in the pioneering works originally associated with the absolutist position (for example, Rowntree 1910). They contend that, ultimately, all conceptions of poverty are relative as it is impossible to detach even the subsistence needs from the customs and conventions of the society in which they emerge (Veit-Wilson 1986). This contention, however, misses the subtle but important distinction drawn between 'needs' and 'need satisfiers' (Max-Neef 1989; Doyal and Gough 1991).

In their theory of human need, Doyal and Gough (1991) define needs as requirements to avoid serious harm (that is, impaired participation in any form of life) and distinguish between core and intermediate needs. The latter denotes the pre-conditions for the satisfaction of core needs, that is, health and critical autonomy, and includes adequate nutrition, clean water, protective housing, non-hazardous work and physical environment, appropriate healthcare, basic education, security in childhood, significant primary relationships and economic and physical security. The need satisfiers are, however, of a different order; they represent the goods, services, activities and relationships required to fulfil the core as well as intermediate needs. Doyal and Gough purport that while need satisfiers are context-dependent, both core and intermediate needs are universally applicable to all human beings regardless of where and when they live. The authors recognise that their list of intermediate needs is not definitive and allow room for refinement provided that the newly identified ones are also universally applicable.

The 'dual strategy' that Gough (2017) proposes to use for identification of need satisfiers through combining expert and public views can also be applied in refining the list. Consequently, by retaining the idea of 'absolute need' as separate from 'relative need satisfiers', the theory allows a middle ground to be taken within the debates concerning the definition of poverty. It not only enables the conceptual distinction between poverty and inequality to be maintained, but also makes it possible to define and measure poverty in a cross-nationally applicable manner while remaining sensitive to people's subjectivities and contextual circumstances. Based on this nuanced understanding of human need, this study construes (migrant) poverty as the lack of resources to obtain the need satisfiers required to avoid serious harm, or impaired participation in any form of life.

Moving on to the question of poverty measurement, both absolutist and relativist perspectives have been utilised to address this issue. Poverty is initially measured purely in monetary terms to track inadequacy of income or consumption. Income poverty lines are often set at an absolute minimum (for example, the World Bank's extreme poverty line of $1.90 a day) or at a certain percentage of the median disposable income adjusted for household size (that is, equivalised). Most commonly, 50 or 60 per cent of the median is taken as the cut-off (see, for example, EUROSTAT 2010; OECD 2019). Income thresholds are usually determined in a top-down, 'objective' manner, and to a lesser extent based on people's views and feelings about income adequacy (see, for example, Flik and Van Praag 1991 for a review of subjective poverty lines including the Leyden Poverty Line). Consumption poverty lines are, on the other hand, determined by estimating the cost of food and/or non-food expenditure considered essential for human existence (see, for example, UNSTATS 2005 for a review). The relative (dis) advantages of using income- and consumption-based measures are extensively debated. There are, however, generic limitations that apply to all monetary approaches regardless of whether they draw on income or expenditure (see also Wisor 2012 for a critique). At best, these approaches capture elements of poverty linked to commodified consumption within a single indicator. They hence remain insensitive to differential human needs and fail to represent those that cannot be attached a monetary value (for example, poor air quality, hazardous and insecure working conditions and lack of access to state welfare services). In an attempt to overcome their shortcomings, multi-dimensional approaches are now being devised and applied across the globe, two of which have been of particular influence within and outside academia.

The first is derived from Townsend's (1979) relative deprivation perspective, which advocates measuring poverty objectively, using expert judgement about prevailing standards of living. Many of its proponents depart from his original position by adopting a 'consensual' method that incorporates public perceptions of necessities. Two versions of this method are worthy of mention: one is originally designed and applied by Mack and Lansley (1983) and the other by Halleröd (1994). The former draws on the majority view to determine socially perceived necessities, and defines the poor as those who want but do not have the items perceived by 50 per cent of the population as necessities (for its recent applications, see, for example, Gordon et al 2000; Nandy and Pomati 2014; Gordon 2015; Guio et al 2017; Gordon et al 2019). The latter version weighs the initially selected list of necessities, based on the proportion of population that views the item as a necessity (Halleröd 1994, 1995).

A detailed evaluation of the consensual method and its main variants can be found in Eroğlu (2007); hence, only their strengths and weaknesses will be summarised here. These studies are noteworthy in their efforts to integrate social perceptions into multi-dimensional poverty measurement and to produce nationally applicable deprivation indices that are additive, reliable and valid. They are, however, fraught with certain limitations. First, the selected necessities are mostly restricted to consumer items. Second, the majoritarian thinking dominates the ways in which social perceptions of necessities are factored into the index design, ignoring the potential mismatch between practices and priorities of the majority and the bearers of poverty (Veit-Wilson 1986). Third, the separate analysis of wants and affordability can potentially lead to invalid results, considering that people are not necessarily the best arbiters of their needs as they are likely to conflate needs and wants, and adapt their preferences to the conditions of their life circumstances (Marcuse 1964; Sen 1987; Doyal and Gough 1991). Finally, since these methods endeavour to identify necessities (hence, poverty indicators) purely from a relativist standpoint by drawing on the 'bottom-up' views of the public, their ability to meet the measurement invariance criterion required for cross-national comparison is potentially compromised.

The deprivation-based approach the author of this book developed and applied in her earlier research on multi-dimensional poverty addresses the first three limitations as well as presenting significant potential for overcoming the fourth (Eroğlu 2004, 2007, 2011). This approach 'objectively' identifies necessities linked to three dimensions of poverty (that is, monetary, consumption- and work-related), and then, resorts to subjective perceptions of respondents to identify a core of necessities and estimate their relative weights through a unique application of factor analysis. This approach is distinct from the works of Townsend (1979), Mack and Lansley (1985) and Halleröd (1994) conceptually as well as methodologically. The main points of distinction are as follows: a) following Doyal and Gough (1991), it recognises the universality of human needs; b) it takes a middle ground between the objectivity–subjectivity continuum by combining expert and public views about necessities; c) it identifies core necessities in a way that is less susceptible to arbitrary selection; d) it differentiates between choice and constraint more reliably than separate explorations of wants and affordability; and e) it represents the views of every respondent, not only those of the majority, in determining necessities and their corresponding weights. The result is a theoretically more sophisticated instrument than similar indices used previously; however, it will not be possible to adapt and apply this approach to the exploration of migrant poverty due to data unavailability.

The second most influential approach to multi-dimensional poverty draws on Sen's (1993, 1999) capability perspective. Among many others, it underpins the Human Development Index (for example, UNDP 1990) as well as the subsequent Multi-Dimensional Poverty Index co-produced by the Oxford Poverty and Human Development Initiative and the United Nations Development Programme (for example, Alkire and Santos 2010; UNDP 2010). Sen (1993) conceives of capabilities as potential 'functionings' (that is, states of being and activities) that a person values and has freedom to achieve, and includes literacy, eating well and longevity among the valuable functionings. However, his refusal to prescribe a list of core capabilities has raised serious concerns about the operationalisability of this approach. For example, Gough et al (2007) argue that even if capabilities are restricted to *actual* functionings, the scope for valuable functionings still remains too wide, and in the absence of a theory-driven list of core capabilities, it would be difficult to agree upon any functionings beyond the basics. Sen's followers have attempted to develop such a list and the one produced by Nussbaum (2000, 2006) has been most influential. She spells out ten categories of capabilities, of which three are deemed core: bodily integrity, affiliation and practical reason. Her list is commended for providing a richer portrayal of human flourishing than Sen (Gough et al 2007). However, as pointed out by Gough (2017), a) the core capabilities put forward by Nussbaum are already covered by the human needs theory under the rubrics of health, participation and critical autonomy, and b) in justifying her claims about their universality, she inescapably resorts to the idea of need without explaining what it means.

Thus, it is needless to adopt the individualistic and ambiguous language of capabilities when the collectivist notion of human needs provides a sufficient basis for developing a theoretically sound, empirically operationalisable and generally applicable way of measuring poverty from a monetary or a multi-dimensional perspective without losing sight of people's subjectivities and contextual circumstances. A recent confirmation of this is the study by Goedemé et al (2015), which successfully combines Doyal and Gough's theory of human needs with a 'dual strategy' to produce cross-nationally comparable reference budgets for 26 EU countries that cover *monetised* need satisfiers subsumed under four intermediate need categories: that is, food, housing, healthcare and personal care. While the resulting budgets would only allow for monetary measurement of poverty, the underpinning theory and methodology remain potentially applicable to multi-dimensional poverty measurement. Due to data constraints, the author will only be able to exploit this potential in her future work.

Despite the aforementioned shortcomings of the prevailing perspectives on multi-dimensional poverty, it should be submitted that multi-dimensional approaches retain a greater capacity to provide a comprehensive representation of poverty than monetary methods of measurement. However, the latter constitutes the predominantly adopted approach within the international migration literature examining the poverty of migrants and/or their descendants. The most commonly used thresholds are income-based. Only the work of Hansen and Wahlberg (2009) adopts a consumption poverty line, derived from minimum needs standards set out by the Swedish National Board of Health and Welfare. The overwhelming majority of the single case studies of Canada and the US adopt the official income poverty lines designated federally or by the National Statistics Office (Jensen 1991; Oropesa and Landale 1997; Chapman and Bernstein 2003; Van Hook et al 2004; Fleury 2007; Sullivan and Ziegert 2008; Thomas 2011; Emeka 2016; Young et al 2018). A small group of single and cross-country studies focussing on the advanced economies in Europe, North America and/or Australia take 50 per cent of the equivalised disposable household income as the cut-off (Galloway and Aaberge 2005; Picot et al 2008; Kesler 2015; Jakobsen and Pedersen 2017; Eugster 2018). However, a major part of the literature exploring migrant poverty in European context(s) adopt the threshold set out within the EURO 2020 Strategy (EUROSTAT 2010), according to which migrants are deemed poor if they fall below 60 per cent of the equivalent median income of the country in which they reside (Blume et al 2007; Lelkes 2007; Galloway et al 2009; Lelkes and Zólyomi 2011; Muñozoz de Bustillo and Anton 2011; Obucina 2014; Hooijer and Picot 2015; Heizmann and Böhnke 2016; Bárcena-Martìn and Pérez-Moreno 2017; Carpio 2017).

Only a few of the existing works approach migrant poverty from a multi-dimensional viewpoint (Pi Alperin 2008; Berti et al 2014; Corrigan et al 2014; Arcagni et al 2019). To briefly describe the main features of the measurement instruments used in these studies, Arcagni et al (2019) construct a deprivation scale, based on four key attributes: that is, living (accommodation) arrangements, receipt of economic aid from relatives or institutions, medical treatment renunciation and equivalent net family income. The measure developed by Berti et al (2014) includes 26 deprivation items linked to seven key dimensions: namely, basic lifestyle, consumer durables, housing arrangements, financial situation, environment, work and health. Corrigan's (2014) study draws on seven of the deprivation items derived originally by Whelan and Maître's (2007) study from EU-SILC: that is, the lack of car, phone and PC ownership and the inability to have regular healthy meals, to heat the home, to cope with unexpected expenses and to go on a one-week holiday every year. Finally, Pi Alperin (2008) measures poverty based on 16 items subsumed under four key dimensions: basic and secondary non-monetary deprivation, housing and equivalent household income. Clearly, considerable divergence is evident among these instruments in their coverage, labelling and clustering of poverty dimensions and/or indicators, which reflects a generic problem with the wider multi-dimensional poverty research. This problem arises either from the absence of an underpinning theory or from the lack of agreement over a clear-cut theoretical framework to inform instrument design.

The existing multi-dimensional approaches to migrant poverty employ a fuzzy estimation technique that moves away from the dichotomous analysis of poverty, that is, using a cut-off point to distinguish between the poor and the non-poor. This technique is considered to yield more realistic estimates of the degree and diffusion of poverty (Arcagni et al 2019). However, much of the current research continues to draw on the poor versus non-poor distinction to determine the incidence of poverty, that is, the poverty rate. A sub-group of these studies also estimates its intensity and severity determined by the poverty gap and squared poverty gap measures (Lelkes and Zólyomi 2011; Muñozoz de Bustillo and Anton 2011; Kesler 2015).

Either from a monetary or a multi-dimensional perspective, the above-reviewed literature provides an 'objective' assessment of migrant poverty. There is only one study by Sabates-Wheeler et al (2008) that relies solely on a subjective measure to compare the poverty status of migrants and their counterparts remaining in the country of origin. This study conceives of migrants and stayers as poor if they feel their household income is barely sufficient or insufficient to meet basic needs. However, considering the absence of clarity and consistency around the composition of basic needs, this approach is unlikely to produce a credible estimate of migrant poverty.

Consequently, recognising the plurality of human needs, the author of this book subscribes to the idea of measuring poverty from a multi-dimensional perspective by integrating the expert and public views about human needs and need satisfiers. However, the construction of such a measure requires extensive data collection, and the 2000 Families Survey on which this book is based is unable to meet this requirement. Disposable household income is the only aspect of the Survey that that would allow poverty to be estimated 'objectively'; that is why a monetary approach had to be adopted here. Following the general tendency displayed by most European research on migrant poverty, this book will utilise the EUROSTAT (2010) threshold set at 60 per cent of the equivalent median income of the country of residence. The steps taken to produce the thresholds for each country covered in this study are explained in Chapter Four.

A resource-based approach to migrant poverty

Four central questions arise from the definition provided above for migrant poverty:

1. What resources are key to need satisfaction?
2. Through which economic actions are these resources converted into outcomes for poverty?

3. What are the main factors that enable or constrain the availability, management and capacity of these resources to ensure need satisfaction?
4. How do the processes of international migration interact with these factors?

The existing theorising about migrant poverty and performance lacks the potential to fully answer these questions, except for the resource-based framework that the author of this book adapted from her earlier work on poverty and applied to understanding migrants' economic behaviours (see, for example, Eroğlu 2011, 2013, 2018, 2020, 2021). This framework will be further developed here to provide a holistic explanation for migrant poverty. Before depicting its key features, relevant theories from the international migration field will be evaluated first.

As shown in Chapter Two, migrant poverty literature occasionally frames migrants' educational and social resources in respective terms of human and social capital (Kazemipur and Halli 2001; Heizmann and Böhnke 2016) but without offering a resource typology. The wider literature does in fact typologise migrant resources using variants of the capital approach originally formulated by scholars such as Bourdieu (1986) and Coleman (1988) to investigate the role of human, cultural and/or social capital resources in migrants' economic and social integration into destination contexts (for example, Alba and Nee 2003), or the ways in which these resources are generated through migrant networks (Ryan et al 2015). Some studies deviate from the tendency to use the language of capital but nevertheless come up with similar resource types. In their study of migrant wellbeing, Ryan et al (2008) distinguish between personal, material, social and cultural resources. However, none of the existing typologies provide a comprehensive coverage of the resources potentially accessible to international migrants.

On the question of resource enablers and constraints, the empirical literature may have unearthed a wide range of individual-, household- and country-level forces likely to affect migrant poverty, but as demonstrated in Chapter Two, these tend to be examined in a fragmented and data-driven manner. Moreover, key influences, such as intergenerational family transfers, remain overlooked. Only the wider literature articulates their links with international migration and migrant resources. For example, Nauck (2001) conceives of international migration as a breakpoint that can lead to devaluation or loss of (grand)parental resources such as social capital. The existing theorising in the field is directed more towards understanding the role of the context. As reviewed earlier, migrant poverty studies conceptualise the impact of the work–welfare–conditionality nexus, drawing on ideas put forward, for example, by Sainsbury (2012) and Soysal (2012) to highlight the significance of migrants' legal rights (Corrigan 2014; Eugster 2018; Young et al 2018). Relevant theories from the wider performance literature are more focussed on exploring the potential influence of the context in shaping migrants' and their descendants' assimilation or integration into the mainstream.

The most widely known and used theories include the following. *Modes of incorporation*, developed by Portes (1995), emphasises the importance of three 'contexts of reception' in the economic adaptation of migrants and their descendants into the host society: a) government policies aimed at immigrants, b) civil society and public attitudes towards particular immigrant groups (that is, discrimination and prejudice) and c) ethnic community by virtue of their role in enabling or constraining their resources. Likewise, the *new institutionalist theory of assimilation*, proposed by Alba and Nee (2003), draws attention to the interplay between the resources and purposive actions of migrants and their descendants and the contexts, including institutional structures, cultural beliefs and social networks. Likewise, the *mixed embeddedness approach* typically applied to understanding the entrepreneurial behaviour of migrants and/or their descendants promotes the idea that economic action and outcomes are embedded in social, economic, politico-institutional and spatial contexts (for example, Kloosterman 2000; Rath 2000; Rekers and van Kempen 2000; Kloosterman et al 2016). Along the same lines, comparative integration context theory highlights the role of social and political contexts, alongside a range of national and local institutional arrangements within the areas of education, labour market, housing, religion and legislation, in enabling or hindering migrants' and their descendants' participation in and belonging to urban life in destination countries while recognising their agency (Schneider and Crul 2012).

Evidently, some of these theories articulate the link between contextual influences and the resources or economic actions of migrants. However, they either do not spell out what those resources are (for example, Portes 1995), or when they do, they offer a restricted resource typology (for example, Alba and Nee 2003). Neither do they identify the key economic actions through which resources are converted into (un)successful outcomes. It is precisely this connection between migrant resources and economic behaviours (or livelihoods) that is claimed to be missing from the existing conceptualisations of the relationship between international migration and development (De Haas 2010).

It is clear from the above review that there exists no single theory that brings together all the core influences upon migrant poverty while articulating their relationships with migrants' resources and economic actions. The proposed model is intended to fill in this theoretical vacuum. Let us now turn to summarising its key components.

The model examines (migrant) poverty in terms of the relationships described in Figure 3.1. While recognising the agency of individuals in managing resources and converting them into economic actions with potential outcomes for poverty, it draws particular attention to the core micro- and macro-level influences likely to affect their economic

Figure 3.1: A resource-based approach to poverty and migration

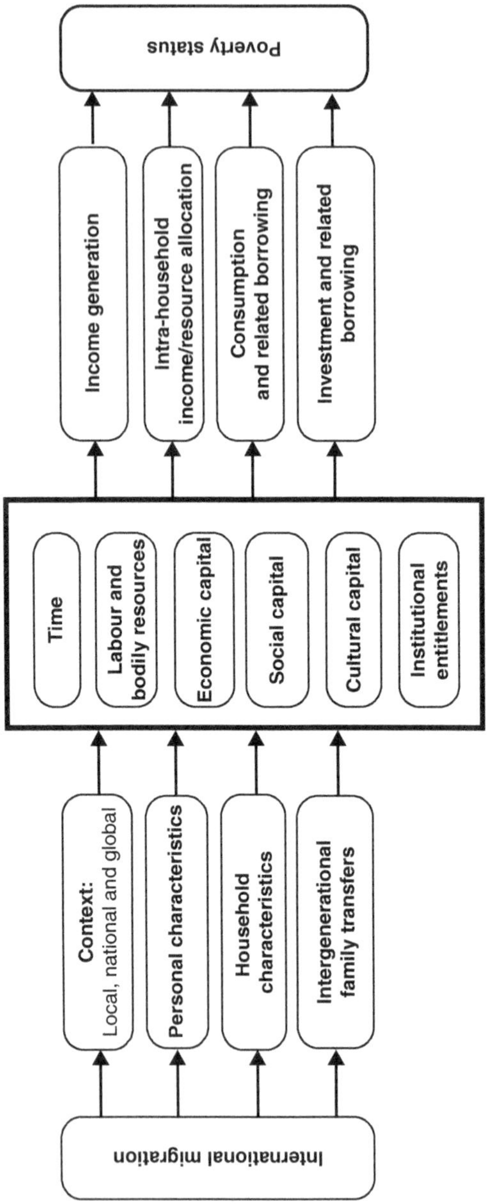

Source: Adapted from Eroğlu (2021)

behaviours and poverty status by virtue of their role in (re) shaping resource portfolios.

The model identifies four core areas within which economic actions can be developed: that is, income generation, intra-household (income/resource) allocation, consumption and investment (including related borrowing). *Income generation* embraces formal and informal activities in which individuals and their households engage to obtain a monetary income. *Intra-household allocation* primarily concerns the distribution of income between different areas of savings and expenditure for the overall household and its individual members. It can also be extended to the allocation of anything that comes into the household in kind. *Consumption* covers a range of activities situated on a continuum from commodified (that is, paid for) to non-commodified (that is, unpaid for), indicating the degree of monetisation within the consumption practices individuals and their households engage in to gain access to goods and services, along with any borrowing undertaken for consumption purposes. *Investment* refers to those practices through which individuals and their households create financial and non-financial assets. Examples of these include generation of 'surplus' income, taking an investment loan from formal or informal credit sources and redeployment of previously acquired assets. Although, in theory, investment is considered as separate from insurance, in real life, the boundaries between the two can become rather blurred, especially where private forms of insurance are concerned.

Resources are viewed as capacities that can be mobilised within the above behavioural areas in their own right or in combination with others to generate material and immaterial benefits (for example, information, money, assets, goods, services and moral support) from various sources, including the market, the state, the household/family and the wider community. The key resources that are potentially accessible to the individuals and their households are grouped into six types: that is, time, labour and bodily resources, economic, cultural and social capital and institutional entitlements. Time and labour resources are self-explanatory, but the others need further depiction to clarify their boundaries. The *bodily resources* are separated from *labour resources* in recognition of the possibility that they can be deployed without exerting labour power (for example, the sale of one's organs for a passport). The notion of *cultural capital* is used in the same way as Bourdieu (1986) to indicate skills, knowledge and qualifications obtained formally through schooling and informally through personal life experiences. The term *economic capital* is also taken from Bourdieu to refer to financial and non-financial assets that can immediately and directly be converted into money. The concept of *social capital* is defined in a narrower sense than Bourdieu to denote relatively durable relations formed inside and outside markets. This is akin to Pizzorno's (2001) use of the term, which, however, excludes market-based contacts. *Institutional entitlements* embrace rights of access to various monetary and non-monetary benefits (for example, cash, assets, goods and services) that are bestowed by governmental and non-governmental bodies. These entitlements, for example, regulate the terms and conditions under which individuals are allowed access to the labour, asset and financial markets, the state (welfare) and the voluntary sector organisations.

The model does not assume that having more resources will necessarily reduce poverty given the fine distinction it draws between the availability of resources and their capacity to deliver benefits. By this distinction, it is implied that people may have resources but still be poor, not simply because they are unable to manage them effectively and efficiently, but because the resources accessible to them remain limited in their capacity to deliver benefits. The model identifies four key factors that can enhance or restrain the benefit delivery capacity of the resources as well as their availability: a) personal features, b) household characteristics, c) the context and d) intergenerational family transfers. There are myriad ways in which these factors can shape the configuration of one's resource portfolio. It is beyond the scope of this book to represent the entire set of possibilities. Only their potential effects on some of the migrant resources will be illustrated below.

Personal features include age, sex, ethnicity, migration origins, history and (legal) status. Let us exemplify their likely effects on institutional entitlements. Some of the entitlements to welfare can be age- and gender-specific. Migrants themselves or their ancestors and descendants may be required to have a history in the destination country to become eligible for certain civic, social and political rights, including those governing terms and conditions of access to work and welfare. Migrants from certain ethnic backgrounds and origins can be treated differently by receiving governments in terms of the extent to which they can benefit from such rights. Access to institutional entitlements is completely denied to illegal migrants, while the holders of citizenship and refugee status tend to be granted varied access.

Household characteristics consist of size, composition/structure and stage in the life cycle. This set of factors is particularly important in terms of its potential to determine the amount of labour resources available to the unit at a given point in time. However, there are other ways in which they can be influential. For example, the presence of 'natives' in the household was shown earlier to be inversely associated with migrant poverty (Bárcena-Martìn and Pérez-Moreno 2017). 'Natives' may well be making a positive difference through enhancing migrants' cultural and social capital resources in ways that reduce their exposure to discrimination.

The *context* encompasses a wide range of influences operating at the local, national and global levels. Building upon past conceptualisations of the context and its role in shaping migrant poverty and performance, the main influences are grouped under three broad and interrelated categories: a) the conditions of the labour, asset and financial markets, b) government policy, especially concerning the areas of employment, social welfare and immigration and

c) institutional racism and public attitudes to migrants. To illustrate, these forces can affect migrants' access to paid work and returns on their labour resources. For example, government policy and systemic racism embedded within government institutions could mean tightened conditions of access to the labour market, potentially leading to unemployment. Even when migrants are legally entitled to work, they can still be blocked from enjoying certain job opportunities (for example, salaried positions commensurate with their educational qualifications) due to discrimination and prejudice. Such a mismatch between their occupational and educational status is likely to bring lower returns on their formal cultural capital.

Intergenerational family transfers or transmissions refer to endowments passed on from other family generations in the form of beliefs, values, resources and behaviours. Transferable resources can take a variety of shapes and forms linked with economic capital (for example, assets and down payments towards education, house purchases/repairs, business ventures), cultural capital (for example, knowledge, skills and experience) and even social capital (for example, family connections to people in important positions in the opportunity structure). When people are left to their own devices in the market, poor families will most likely transmit fewer, less beneficial resources than the non-poor. This pattern of transmission is unlikely to change unless it is interrupted by substantial state intervention or major life-changing events or processes.

International migration is seen here as one such process that is likely to reconfigure migrants' resources, behaviours and poverty status by changing the local and national contexts in which they operate, some of their personal and household characteristics (for example, national and ethnic identity and household composition) and/or the nature and extent of intergenerational family transfers. As evidenced in Chapter Two, the direction of change may not be as positive as the assimilationists expect.

Overall, the proposed model makes major advances upon earlier versions of the resource-based framework used within the poverty and livelihood research (for example, Swift 1989; Moser 1998; Eroğlu 2004, 2011; Bebbington et al 2007); a detailed discussion of these can be found in Eroğlu (2011, 2013). The model is also a significant improvement upon other relevant approaches developed and applied previously within the wider international migration literature. As well as offering a theoretically sophisticated resource portfolio with conceptual clarity and empirical applicability, it paints a more complete picture of the resources that are key to (migrant) poverty. It also provides a more comprehensive representation of the complex casual paths between poverty and international migration by recognising not only the contextual influences upon household resources and economic behaviours but also the factors operating at the individual and household levels and across family generations. Furthermore, by conceptualising the interplays between migration, migrant resources and economic behaviours (or livelihoods), the model establishes the missing link of which De Haas (2010) speaks.

Conclusion: towards research hypotheses

Drawing together the theoretical ideas and past research findings presented earlier, this section will set out research hypotheses about the impoverished predicament of the populations studied in this book. As will be detailed in Chapter Four, the target populations consist of three family generations of migrants from Turkey to Europe, who are currently living in their destination countries, including Austria, Belgium, Denmark, France, Germany, Sweden and the Netherlands, and those who moved (back) to Turkey, along with their 'non-migrant' comparators who did not leave their origins for longer than a year. For sake of brevity, these population groups will respectively be referred to as the 'settlers', 'returnees' and 'stayers'.

One might expect the settlers in Europe to fare the best, thinking that the conditions of the European labour markets are more favourable than they are in Turkey. While there is an element of truth in this, the European labour markets have witnessed considerable deterioration in pay and working conditions, especially since the financial crisis in 2008. Migrants are shown to have been hit the hardest by the recent crisis and faced with increased unemployment, insecure employment and 'a perverse cycle of exclusion', pushing them into poverty (for example, Carpio 2017). The European studies on migrant poverty rarely speak explicitly about systemic racism and public hostility towards migrants, yet evidence shows that nearly half of the Europeans are against migration from poorer countries (Blinder and Markaki 2018). Therefore, systemic racism is highly likely to persist as a structural influence that leads to increased poverty by discriminating especially against those groups of migrants who originated from economically less developed, non-EU countries. Such discriminatory practices may, for example, result in unemployment or lead to a mismatch between educational and occupational status, bringing lower returns from their cultural capital accumulations unless they are able to bypass it through engagement in lucrative small businesses, but even then, they are likely to trade this with occupational prestige (Eroğlu 2018). Given these considerations, it is unlikely that the European labour markets will give the settlers a significant advantage over their counterparts living in Turkey – especially the returnees, most of whom will be from older age groups with substantial asset holdings in Turkey (Eroğlu 2021). Their asset accumulations may well act as a buffer against poverty. They may also have accrued a pension or made savings during their time abroad. However small these are, when converted into Turkish lira, they may still help them stay above the monetary poverty threshold set for Turkey. Consequently, across all European destinations, the settlers are expected to be the most impoverished whereas the returnees are to be the least (Hypothesis 1).

The settlers living in more generous welfare states are not expected to fare better, either (Hypothesis 2). This is fundamentally because they fall under the category of 'unwanted migrants' from outside the EU27 who are denied the benefits offered to their native counterparts (Hooijer and Picot 2015). It is highly probable that underneath such exclusion lies the racism that pervades large segments of the European societies and institutions. It would hence be rather optimistic to expect a substantial decline in public hostility towards the younger generations. Therefore, it remains unlikely that the settlers from subsequent family generations will fare significantly better than their first generation, stayer or returnee counterparts (Hypothesis 3).

In an environment where non-EU migrants are excluded from the generosity of established welfare states, it is improbable that the settlers in Europe will be able to prevent intergenerational transmission of poverty to a significant extent. The same is also likely for the stayers living in a context where a fully developed welfare state is non-existent. The returnees' 'faith' may, however, differ from the other two, given the assets they have accumulated in Turkey, possibly through converting the economic capital they have generated (for example, in the form of savings) during their time abroad. Thus, the settlers and the stayers are expected not to be as successful as the returnees in preventing the transmission of poverty across family generations (Hypothesis 4).

FOUR

Researching migrant poverty

This chapter presents the methodological approach taken to empirically investigate migrant poverty. It starts by depicting the key characteristics of the target population and the sample to demonstrate its appropriateness for the exploration of migrant poverty from a multi-site and intergenerational perspective. This is followed by a presentation of the survey design and implementation, along with the methods, techniques and instruments used in sampling, data collection and analysis. The chapter ends with a detailed exposition of the dependent and independent variables and their links to the resource-based model.

Target migrant population and the sample

The research base for this study is the 2000 Families Survey, primarily interested in the guest-worker movement from Turkey to Europe. This process began in the early 1960s with Turkey's signing of bilateral agreements with many Northern and Western European countries that had sought to tackle the labour shortages they had experienced in the aftermath of the Second World War by recruiting labour from Eastern and Southern Europe. About one million people, typically men, left Turkey to work in the mining, manufacturing and construction industries of these countries, and came to form the largest guest-worker population in Europe (Akgündüz 2008). A large portion of the movers was from the rural parts of the country, and the five regions (that is, Acıpayam, Akçaabat, Emirdağ, Kulu and Şarkışla) screened by the Survey remain among the areas that witnessed some of the highest levels of outmigration at the time (Güveli et al 2015). The guest-worker agreements ended with the economic crisis in the mid-1970s; yet migration from Turkey to Europe has continued to date for a range of reasons, from family formation and unification to education, employment and political asylum (Güveli et al 2017). Today, approximately five million people with origins in Turkey are estimated to live in Europe spanning multiple destinations and generations (Güveli et al 2017).

The Survey charted family genealogies of male ancestors who moved during guest-worker years and their counterparts who remained in the country of origin up to the fourth generation. This involved screening the aforementioned regions to identify 'migrant' and 'non-migrant' families. The eligibility criteria for the former were to have a male ancestor who a) might be dead or alive, b) was or would have been between the ages of 65 and 90, c) grew up in the region, d) moved to Europe over the guest-worker period and e) stayed there for at least five years. The same criteria were used for non-migrant families, except that their male ancestors must have stayed in Turkey rather than moving to Europe. The respondents sampled from these families, however, do not necessarily share the same gender or migration status as their male ancestors. They were divided into three groups: a) 'settlers' who have been residing in Europe for a year or more, b) 'returnees' who went (back) to Turkey after having spent at least a year there and c) 'stayers' who had never left Turkey for more than a year.

Overall, the Survey embraces the first male labour migrants from Turkey to Europe and their migrant and native-born descendants, along with the members of families with 'non-migrant' ancestors who moved subsequently. Hence, it not only represents the typical features of the guest-workers and their families, but also captures a good portion of the 'Turkish' diaspora in Europe. By focussing on this significant minority group, the book seizes a perfect opportunity to investigate migrant poverty from a multi-site and intergenerational perspective.

Research questions

The empirical part of this book examines the monetary poverty profiles of the three family generations of settler and returnee migrants as compared with their stayer counterparts to answer the following research questions:

1. Do the settlers and returnees differ significantly from the stayers in the extent to which they experience monetary poverty?
2. (a) Are subsequent generations more or less likely to be monetarily impoverished than their male ancestors? (b) Do significant generational differences exist between the three groups?
3. (a) Are the adult children with poor parents significantly more likely to experience monetary poverty than those with non-poor parents? (b) To what extent do adult children from the three groups differ in the extent to which they escape parental monetary poverty?
4. What do any of the observed differences between groups and across generations tell us about the poverty consequences of international migration?

Research hypotheses

As expounded in Chapter Three, the following hypotheses will be tested in this study:

1. The risk of exposure to poverty is expected to be the highest for the settlers and the lowest for the returnees.
2. The settlers residing in countries with more generous welfare states are unlikely to fare better than their counterparts living under less generous welfare regimes.
3. The settlers from subsequent generations are unlikely to fare any better than their first generation, stayer and returnee counterparts.
4. Intergenerational transmission of poverty is likely to remain strong among all groups, except for the returnees.

Selection criteria, screening and sampling

The 2000 Families Survey developed and applied an innovative technique for screening the five high migrant-sending regions to identify the migrant and non-migrant families that met the aforementioned eligibility criteria. A sampling quota of 4:1 was applied to ensure that 80 per cent of the respondents were selected from 'migrant' families and the remaining 20 per cent from 'non-migrant' families. The regions were screened using a clustered probability sampling technique. One hundred primary sampling units (PSUs) with random starting points were drawn from the Turkish Statistical Institute's (TURKSTAT) address register. The size of each PSU was proportional to the estimated population size of the randomly chosen locality. Each PSU was screened through random walk. This involved going to the random starting point and knocking on every door if the locality inhabited less than 1,000 households and on every other door if the number of inhabitants was 1,000 or above. Four migrant families were sampled for every non-migrant. The random walk ended when 60 households were screened or when eight families were recruited.

The screenings were carried out in two stages. First, a pilot study was performed in Şarkışla in the summer of 2010. The remaining four regions were screened in the summer of 2011, during which approximately 21,000 addresses were visited to achieve the target of 400 families per region. The strike rate (that is, the proportion of eligible families) was around one in every 12 households, yielding 1,992 participating families in total.

As summarised below, the Survey used multiple instruments and two modes of interviewing to generate data. Face-to-face interviews were conducted with those who were present in the field while the absentees were interviewed over the phone. The data used in this study are drawn from the personal interviews with male ancestors and their randomly selected male and female descendants aged 18 or above. The sample frame for each family consisted of the living male ancestor, his two children, two adult children of these two children (that is, the male ancestor's grandchildren) and their adult children if any (that is, the male ancestor's great grandchildren). For randomisation, the adults with initials closest to A and Z were selected. The overall response rate was high at 61 per cent, amounting to a total of 5,980 personal interviews with members of three generations nested within 1,770 families. The non-response rate due to reasons other than non-contact (for example, refusal) was similarly low across eligible family members living in Turkey and Europe, at 6 to 8 per cent. However, by the end of the main-stage fieldwork, the non-contact rate for the European sample was observed to be higher by approximately 18 per cent. This imbalance was redressed through additional three-month tracing performed in 2012 to make contact and interview hard-to-reach family members in Europe. The tracing process yielded 515 interviews, increasing the response rate for this group of respondents by about 20 per cent. The figure of 5,980 includes the respondents recruited through additional tracing.

Data collection instruments

Multiple instruments have been developed and administered using face-to-face and phone interview modes to generate the Survey database. The family tree module was administered on a well-informed member of the male ancestor's lineage (often turning out to be the doorstep informant) to map out the complete genealogy of the male ancestor's children, grandchildren and great grandchildren for 1,992 families. The module generated basic demographic information about 49,000 family members. A proxy questionnaire was conducted, again with a well-informed family member, to obtain basic information about the socio-economic and migration backgrounds of all lineage members aged 18 and above. As a result, proxy information for about 19,666 adults was obtained. Personal interviews administered on living male ancestors and randomly selected family members aged 18 or above generated in-depth information about the resources, behaviours, values and beliefs of 5,980 individuals nested within 1,770 families. This book draws on personal interview data – the only source containing income information.[1]

Data analysis

A series of multi-variable analyses were performed to examine migrant poverty in terms of the relationships described in Figure 3.1, but without entering the behavioural realm. The overarching aim in conducting these analyses was not to uncover all possible drivers of migrant poverty but to provide fresh insight into the poverty consequences of international migration.

The ideal would have been to apply the multi-level modelling technique to ascertain the extent to which any observed variation was attributable to the micro- (individual, household and generational) and macro-level (contextual) forces. This was, however, not possible due to the number of studied countries with sufficient cases being lower than 15 (that is, eight including Turkey). Instead, probit models of monetary

1 The author used personal data from this Survey in her previous publications focusing on migrants' economic behaviours (Eroğlu 2018, 2020, 2021).

poverty were estimated to conduct three-way comparisons between the settlers, stayers and returnees along with a sub-analysis involving only the settlers.

The three groups have been compared aggregately as well as separately, using data obtained from the entire and split samples. Two pooled (or aggregate) probit models were estimated to answer distinct research questions. Model 1 was developed to evaluate the consequences of migration for monetary poverty (R.Q.1 and R.Q.4) and to document generational trends (R.Q.2a). Model 2 was designed specifically to explore the extent to which monetary poverty was transmitted from parents to adult children (R.Q.3a), using dyads established between parents and their own children. Dyads describe a relationship between a pair of individuals. Here, members of the second and third generations were linked to their fathers/mothers to determine parental monetary poverty levels. Since no information is available on the male ancestors' parental income, a dyad could not be formed between him and his parents, which is why Model 2 excludes the first generation.

Two sets of separate probit models were also estimated to determine the extent to which observed generational trends in monetary poverty and its transmission across family generations varied across the settlers, returnees and stayers, and thereby, to shed further light upon poverty outcomes of migration (R.Q.2b, 3b and 4). There is controversy surrounding the use of logit and probit for separate group comparisons. Among others, Mood (2010) infamously claims that they cannot be meaningfully compared since the effect sizes depend upon unobserved heterogeneity, variable across samples, groups and points in time. While acknowledging that such an effect exists, Buis (2015: 10) contends that this is a desirable feature of logit if one is to consider the dependent variable, or probability, as 'an assessment of how likely it is that an event occurs'. He goes on to suggest that

> within groups … we are more certain the predicted probabilities can get closer to zero or one, so there is more

> room for a variable to have an effect. Logistic regression coefficients have exactly this property, [and] this property of logistic regression ensures that a comparison of odds ratios give an accurate description of the difference in effects across groups. (Buis 2015: 10)

This study follows Buis's position, allowing probit coefficients to be used for group comparisons as estimates of probability that are an artefact of another binary response model similar to logit.

Further analyses performed with the sub-group of settlers specifically investigates the hypothesised relationship between poverty and welfare generosity, alongside other influences that only apply to migrant populations. The exploration of this relationship could not be extended to the stayers or the returnees due to the unavailability of a welfare generosity score for Turkey.

Finally, all probit models estimated are cluster-corrected to take account of within-family association. Let us now turn to introduce the variables built into the models.

The *dependent variable* remains the same across all probit estimations. It would have been ideal to develop a multi-dimensional measure to capture the non-monetary aspects of poverty as well. This was, however, not feasible due to data constraints. Instead, a monetary poverty measure was constructed, based on the following question: Thinking of all the people living in your household and all sources of income, including earnings, pensions, benefits and investments, what is the total annual income that is at the disposal of your household? The Survey asks about the amount of income and its currency in separate questions. Of 5,960[2] eligible respondents from the first, second or third generation, 4,436

2 Twelve cases had to be dropped because of their current residence being in a non-EU country other than Turkey. A further eight were from the fourth generation; they were also removed from the final analyses due to their low number. This is why the sample size fell from 5,980 to 5,960.

individuals answered both questions, yielding a remarkably high item-response rate of 74.4 per cent.

Nonetheless, auxiliary probit analyses were carried out to check whether the missing income data had been distributed randomly. As can be seen from Table 4.1, the aggregate analyses performed with the entire sample revealed no significant differences between the reporters and non-reporters of income in terms of age, sex or education. However, the likelihood of generating missing information proved to be significantly greater for the settlers in Europe than the stayers in Turkey and lower for those coming from migrant families. Having said this, the missing cases appear to be randomly distributed across the settlers, given the absence of significant variation within this group of migrants in terms of age, sex, education or position in the family genealogy (see Table 4.1).

The monetary poverty measure was created in six steps. First, all household incomes were checked to see whether the reported currency matched that of the respondents' current country of residence. Eurostat (2018) annual average exchange rates were used to convert the non-matching cases into the country currency, considering the year of interview. Second, the household incomes were equivalised, based on the OECD's square root scale to ensure comparability across households with different sizes. Third, since the interviews were conducted between 2010 and 2012, the equivalised household incomes had to be adjusted for inflation, using the country's CPI figures for the years 2010 and 2011 (IMF 2018). Fourth, they were checked for outliers on a per country basis and the outliers were removed, using Hoaglin and Iglewicz's (1987) formula. Consequently, 71 per cent of the entire sample was retained. Fifth, the monetary poverty thresholds were calculated for each country, using 60 per cent of the median equivalent disposable household income as the cut-off. In identifying the cut-offs, the 2012 median disposable household income figures, estimated

Table 4.1: Missing case analyses: household income

	Aggregate sample	Settlers in Europe
Migrant ancestor (a)	–0.14 (0.51) **	–0.21 (0.11)
Individual migration status (b)		
Settlers in Europe	0.40 (0.04) ***	Not applicable
Returnees to Turkey	–0.06 (0.07)	Not applicable
Family generations (c)		
G2	–0.08 (0.13)	–0.19 (0.18)
G3	0.04 (0.14)	–0.04 (0.20)
Age (d)		
Below 25	0.28 (0.15)	0.31 (0.23)
25–45	0.12 (0.14)	0.12 (0.21)
46–65	0.22 (0.13)	0.11 (0.19)
Sex (e)	–0.04 (0.04)	0.05 (0.06)
Highest education (f)		
Primary	–0.17 (0.11)	–0.09 (0.18)
Lower secondary	–0.13 (0.12)	–0.10 (0.19)
Higher secondary	–0.16 (0.12)	–0.06 (0.19)
Lower tertiary or above	–0.20 (0.12)	–0.07 (0.20)
Intercept	–0.67 (0.12)	–0.26 (0.21)
Observations	5,380	2,141
Pseudo R^2	0.03	0.01

Notes: Probit estimations of cases with and without household income data. Standard errors in parentheses. * $p < 0.05$, ** $p < 0.01$, *** $p < 0.001$
(a) baseline: non-migrant; **(b)** baseline: stayers in Turkey;
(c) baseline: G1 – first generation; **(d)** baseline: 65+;
(e) baseline: women; **(f)** baseline: primary dropout.

Source: 2000 Families Survey, personal data

using the same equivalisation scale as the one adopted here, were taken as the basis.

Independent and control variables were chosen carefully to reflect the model features given the data; however, aspects of the model that were solely attributable to migrants (for example, time spent in Europe, country nationality or nativity status) could not be incorporated into the three-way comparisons, because otherwise there would have been no observable variation among the stayers; therefore, these attributes had to be studied separately. Table 4.2 provides a full list of the variables employed within the comparative analyses. These are summarised below with reference to the core components of the model corresponding to parts 1 and 2 of Figure 3.1.

Migration-related influences are embodied within the respondents' personal characteristics, represented here by the variables of migrant ancestry and individual migration status along with age, sex, marital status and position in the family genealogy. Due to the substantial age differences within family generations (mean age for G1 = 72, sd = 6; mean for G2 = 43, sd = 9; mean for G3 = 25, sd = 6), age had to be employed as a control to disentangle any generational effect. The ethnicity variable was omitted from the final analyses as it yielded insignificant results with only a 0.044 gain in pseudo R^2, as well as causing significant loss of statistical power by generating 1,066 missing cases.

Household characteristics are indicated by the household size variable. The ideal would have been to compute household dependency ratios, combining information about household size, composition and stage in the domestic life cycle. However, household size had to be employed as a proxy due to the unavailability of data on all family members' ages or employment status. The existing Survey data on partners' employment status could not be included, as its usage would have restricted the study to married and cohabiting respondents and hence caused a significant reduction in sample size.

Table 4.2: Variables used in three-way comparisons and corresponding descriptives

	Variable description	Descriptive statistics
Dependent variables		
Monetary poverty	Relative income poverty based on 60% of the median equivalent disposable household income	
	1 poor	39% (1,646)
	0 non-poor	61% (2,590)
Independent variables		
Migrant ancestry	1 male ancestor is a migrant	81% (4,807)
	0 non-migrant – REF	19% (1,151)
Individual migration status in context	0 returnees to Turkey	16% (921)
	1 stayer in Turkey – REF	45% (2,695)
	2 settlers in Germany	14% (835)
	3 settlers in Netherlands	4% (264)
	4 settlers in France	4% (233)
	5 settlers in Austria	2% (134)
	6 settlers in Belgium	8% (472)
	7 settlers in Denmark	3% (170)
	8 settlers in Sweden	3% (153)
	9 settlers in another EU country	1% (66)
Family generations	1 first generation: G1	18% (1,053)
	2 second generation: G2 – REF	46% (2,713)
	3 third generation: G3	37% (2,192)
Parental monetary poverty	Relative poverty based on 60% of the median equivalent disposable household income	
	1 poor	41% (1,120)
	0 non-poor – REF	59% (1,597)

(continued)

Table 4.2: Variables used in three-way comparisons and corresponding descriptives (continued)

	Variable description	Descriptive statistics
Control variables		
Age	Age in years [17–90]	(5,900 obs; mean = 41; sd = 18)
Sex	1 man 0 women – REF	62% (3,681) 38% (2,275)
Marital status	1 currently married 0 other – REF	71% (4,205) 29% (1,720)
Household size	Number of people living in respondent's household [1–11]	(5,957 obs; mean = 3.3; sd = 1.7)
Highest education	Highest educational qualification achieved: 1 primary dropout 2 primary – REF 3 lower secondary 4 higher secondary 5 lower tertiary or above	 3% (184) 37% (2,040) 14% (787) 27% (1,450) 18% (994)
Non-financial asset holdings	Full or part ownership of land, business and/or house in the current country of residence [0–6]	(5,717 obs; mean = 1.6; sd = 1.7)

Source: 2000 Families Survey, personal data

The extent of intergenerational transmission of poverty was measured, based on a parental monetary poverty indicator that was derived from the dependent variable by linking parents' information to that of their *own* children. As for the context, an attempt has been made to account for possible national-level influences affecting the origin and destination countries by differentiating the respondents according to their current country of residence. Another contextual influence explored here was the level of welfare generosity, but for reasons explained earlier, it could not be integrated into the three-way comparisons. Local-level effects (for example, urban–rural differences), however, remain unexamined due to data constraints.

Turning to the elements of the resource portfolio, the operationalisation of respondents' economic, cultural and social capital is worthy of further discussion as the other resource types (that is, time, labour and institutional entitlements) have been incidentally addressed earlier when speaking about the predictors of age, household size, duration of stay in Europe, country nationality and nativity status. The formal aspects of cultural capital are characterised by the variable of highest educational qualification achieved. The tangible elements of economic capital are represented by the non-financial asset holdings variable, which was generated from six questions asking about business, land and house ownership in Turkey and the destination country, with response categories of 1: 'yes, full ownership'; 2: 'yes, shared ownership' and 3: 'no ownership'. First, these individual variables were recoded to ensure higher scores indicated greater asset ownership (range 0–2). These scores were then added up to create a non-financial asset holdings variable on a six-point scale. The non-financial investments had to be restricted to those held in the country of residence since the Survey did not ask stayers about their assets in Europe. While the returnees were asked about these, the item-response rate proved to be very low at 10 per cent (95 out of 921). Also, a point needs to be made here about the bi-directional nature of the relationship between poverty and asset accumulation. Although the direction of causality may not be fully established through a cross-sectional analysis, the inclusion of non-financial asset holdings in the models is not anticipated to lead to a major endogeneity problem since these assets are most likely to have been generated prior to the reported household income.

As for social capital, although the Survey contains questions about the volume of people's acquaintances and the socio-economic and demographic characteristics of their close contacts, these questions were not asked at the pilot stage. Their usage would have resulted in 806 missing cases and hence produced a significant loss of statistical power. Therefore, a proxy for social capital could not be generated for inclusion within the three-way comparisons.

A full list of the variables employed within the sub-analyses of the settlers is presented in Table 4.3. The additional variables used here are as follows: destination country citizenship was constructed in the same way as Young et al (2018) to incorporate nativity status. Personal migration histories were indicated by the portion of lifetime spent in Europe, which was only moderately correlated with age ($r = 0.438$, $p < 0.001$) and citizenship status ($r = 0.112$, $p < 0.001$). Ethnicity could be included as a control variable owing to the availability of more complete information for the settlers. While the same six questions were used to capture their economic capital resources, the Survey data allowed separate indicators to be developed to represent their non-financial asset accumulations in the origin and the destination. Social capital resources were measured using a six-point scale where the higher scores indicate greater ownership of inter-ethnic friendship ties. Friendship composition was preferred over a variable indicating the portion of inter-ethnic ties among co-workers as not all settlers are in paid work. Besides, an auxiliary analysis performed with the latter variable revealed no significant relationship between monetary poverty and having more inter-ethnic ties at the workplace (probit = -0.04, $p = 0.191$).

Contextual differences in the settlers' poverty status were captured via the destination country variable. The welfare generosity variable was introduced to further 'unpack' the context, and, more specifically, to examine the poverty impact of relevant government policy. The welfare effort index borrowed from Corrigan for this purpose was a reconstruction of Scruggs and Allan's (2006) benefit generosity index where higher scores indicated more generous welfare provision. The following are the welfare effort scores for the countries studied here: Austria (6.34), Belgium (10.74), Denmark (9.95), France (6.05), Germany (7.73), Netherlands (10.87), Sweden (10.03) and other EU countries (Greece [5.23], Italy [3.86], Norway

Table 4.3: Variables used in sub-analyses of settlers and corresponding descriptives

	Variable description	Descriptive statistics
Dependent variable		
Monetary poverty	Relative poverty based on 60% of the median equivalent disposable household income	
	1 poor	47% (714)
	0 non-poor	53% (813)
Independent variables		
Family generations	1 first generation: G1	15% (341)
	2 second generation: G2 – REF	47% (1,084)
	3 third generation: G3	39% (902)
Migrant ancestry	1 respondent's male ancestor is a migrant	93% (2,158)
	0 non-migrant – REF	7% (169)
Lifetime in Europe	Time spent in Europe in proportion to age	(2,251 obs; mean = 0.76; sd = 0.24)
Destination country	1 Germany – REF	36% (835)
	2 Netherlands	11% (264)
	3 France	10% (233)
	4 Austria	6% (134)
	5 Belgium	20% (472)
	6 Denmark	7% (170)
	7 Sweden	7% (153)
	8 Other EU country	3% (66)
Welfare generosity	Welfare effort scores for each destination [3.86–11.79]	(2,330 obs; mean = 8.80; sd = 1.78)
Destination country citizenship	1 non-citizen	40% (915)
	2 native-born citizens	32% (730)
	3 naturalised citizens – REF	28% (640)
Parental monetary poverty	Relative poverty based on 60% of the median equivalent disposable household income	
	1 poor	49% (538)
	0 non-poor – REF	51% (564)

(continued)

Table 4.3: Variables used in sub-analyses of settlers and corresponding descriptives (continued)

	Variable description	Descriptive statistics
Control variables		
Age	Age in years [17–90]	[2,289 obs; mean = 39; sd = 17]
Sex	1 man 0 women – REF	63% (1,465) 37% (861)
Ethnicity	1 Turkish – REF 2 Kurdish 3 other	81% (1,851) 13% (293) 7% (152)
Marital status	1 currently married 0 other – REF	70% (1,613) 30% (702)
Household size	Number of household members	(2327 obs; mean = 3.11; sd = 1.73)
Highest education	1 primary dropout – REF 2 primary 3 lower secondary 4 higher secondary 5 lower tertiary or above	3% (63) 27% (577) 20% (441) 36% (775) 15% (316)
Non-financial asset holdings in Europe	Full or part ownership of land, business and/or house in the destination country [0– 6]	(2,061 obs; mean = 1.03; sd = 1.36)
Non-financial asset holdings in Turkey	Full or part ownership of land, business and/or house in the country of origin [0–6]	[2,226 obs; mean = 1.36; sd = 1.55]
Inter-ethnic friendship ties	Portion of friends with origins in Turkey – a scale of almost all to none [1–6]	[2,258 obs; mode = 1; median = 2; sd = 1.29]

Source: 2000 Families Survey, personal data

[11.79], Switzerland [9.70] and the UK [5.14]) (Corrigan, 2014: 231).

To further examine the contextual differences, auxiliary analyses were performed with two additional variables derived from the two separate indices created by the MIPEX III project team (Huddleston et al 2011). These indices assess the favourability of the receiving country governments' labour market mobility and anti-discrimination policies for migrants. The studied countries achieved the following scores on the labour market mobility index where higher scores indicated adoption of more favourable policies: Austria (56), Belgium (53), Denmark (73), France (49), Germany (77), Netherlands (85), Sweden (100) and other EU countries (Greece [50], Italy [69], Norway [73], Switzerland [53] and the UK [55]). Their anti-discrimination scores were as follows: Austria (40), Belgium (79), Denmark (47), France (77), Germany (79), Netherlands (68), Sweden (88) and other EU countries (Greece [50], Italy [62], Norway [59], Switzerland [31] and the UK [59]). However, neither variable was included within the final analysis as the monetary poverty levels observed for the settlers based in different destination countries proved not to be significantly correlated with the labour market mobility or anti-discrimination scores (see Chapter Five for the results obtained from auxiliary analyses).

As for influences relating to immigration policy, previous studies sought to examine these through a focus on the level of conditionality placed upon migrants with third country nationality in securing long-term residence (LTR) status, for example, using data from the 2006 MIPEX project (Niessen et al 2007), which identifies multiple policy strands concerning migrant integration into 25 EU member states (Corrigan 2014). However, since the great majority of the settlers have been subject to a specific set of LTR conditions imposed upon the guest-workers and their descendants in the years that followed the end of bilateral labour agreements in the early 1970s, the LTR conditionality index derived from the MIPEX project remains to be of little relevance to the migrant population targeted here. The specific conditions imposed upon them are not feasibly quantifiable with the scope of this study; therefore, their poverty impact could not be directly investigated. Nonetheless, some of the immigration policy-related effects could be picked up by means of the destination country citizenship variable.

Conclusion

This chapter outlined the methodological steps taken to shed light upon the poverty consequences of international migration from a unique multi-site and intergenerational perspective. It also demonstrated the ways in which the concepts underpinning this study were operationalised, and the extent to which they could be investigated statistically. In the next chapter, the results obtained from the statistical analyses will be presented.

FIVE

Do migrants fare better than stayers?

This chapter presents and interprets the results obtained from the statistical analyses of the 2000 Families Survey data to shed light upon the poverty impact of international migration for migrants and their descendants. It starts by summarising the key tendencies emerging from the descriptive analyses of the entire sample and the sub-sample of the settlers spread across multiple European destinations. It then outlines the probit results obtained through the comparisons drawn between the settlers, returnees and stayers spanning three family generations. This is followed by a presentation of the results arising from the probit estimations performed with the sub-sample of settlers. The chapter concludes by explaining the narrative behind the statistical findings.

Descriptive statistics

Key descriptive statistics obtained for the entire sample of eligible respondents (N = 5,960) and the sub-group of settlers, excluding the fourth generation (N = 2,327), have already been presented in Tables 4.2 and 4.3, respectively (see Chapter Four). Tables 5.1, 5.2 and 5.3 break down the results further by individual migration status, country of residence and position

Table 5.1: Conditional distributions by individual migration status

	Settlers in Europe	Returnees to Turkey	Stayers in Turkey
Monetarily poor	53% (813)	26% (180)	33% (649)
Migrant male ancestor	93% (2,158)	94% (861)	66% (1,753)
Family generations			
G1	15% (341)	58% (531)	7% (178)
G2	47% (1,084)	33% (304)	49% (1,304)
G3	39% (902)	9% (86)	45% (1,188)
Monetarily poor parents	51% (564)	33% (60)	34% (484)
Age*	39 (17)	59 (18)	37 (15)
Sex: men	63% (1,465)	83% (764)	54% (1,432)
Marital status: married	70% (1,613)	86% (779)	67% (1,794)
Household size*	3.1 (1.7)	2.9 (1.6)	3.6 (1.7)
Highest education			
Primary dropout	3% (63)	7% (54)	3% (66)
Primary	27% (577)	62% (491)	42% (959)
Lower secondary	20% (441)	9% (71)	11% (271)
Higher secondary	36% (775)	11% (87)	24% (582)
Lower tertiary or above	15% (316)	11% (86)	24% (585)
Average education *	3.3 (1.1)	2.6 (1.1)	3.3 (1.3)
Non-financial asset holdings *	1.0 (1.3)	2.9 (1.6)	1.8 (1.6)

Note: * Mean scores. Standard deviations in parenthesis.

Source: 2000 Families Survey, personal data

Table 5.2: Monetary poverty by individual migration status and current country of residence

	Poor	Non-poor
Stayers in Turkey	33% (653)	68% (1,355)
Returnees to Turkey	26% (180)	74% (521)
Settlers in Germany	49% (268)	51% (275)
Settlers in the Netherlands	53% (94)	47% (83)
Settlers in France	46% (64)	54% (76)
Settlers in Austria	67% (66)	33% (32)
Settlers in Belgium	52% (163)	48% (148)
Settlers in Denmark	64% (72)	36% (40)
Settlers in Sweden	60% (59)	40% (40)
Settlers in another EU country	58% (27)	43% (20)
Total	39% (1,646)	61% (2,590)

Source: 2000 Families Survey, personal data

in the family genealogy. The socio-economic and demographic profiles of the settlers, the returnees and the stayers spanning three generations are depicted in Tables 5.1 and 5.3; therefore, they will not be repeated here. In what follows, only the descriptive tendencies concerning their poverty status will be summarised before turning to test their statistical significance. Across the entire sample, 39 per cent of the respondents turned out to be monetarily impoverished. The propensity for monetary poverty proved to be the highest for the settlers in Europe (that is, 53 per cent) and lowest for the returnees (that is, 26 per cent), despite both displaying similar degrees of migrant ancestry. This tendency remains true for all settlers across all European destinations without an exception. With 67 per cent, the settlers in Austria were found to experience monetary poverty to the greatest extent. The lowest level of poverty was observed among those living in France, yet the figure still stays considerably above the average at 46 per cent. France is followed

Table 5.3: Generational distributions by individual migration status

	Settlers in Europe			Returnees to Turkey			Stayers in Turkey		
	G1	G2	G3	G1	G2	G3	G1	G2	G3
Monetarily poor	79%	49%	49%	23%	30%	24%	33%	38%	27%
Migrant male ancestor	–	93%	90%	–	87%	84%	–	67%	74%
Monetarily poor parents	–	53%	50%	–	30%	39%	–	33%	35%
Age*	71 (5)	42 (8)	25 (6)	73 (5)	44 (9)	28 (6)	72 (6)	44 (9)	25 (6)
Sex: men	100%	59%	54%	100%	58%	66%	100%	48%	53%
Marital status: married	95%	87%	40%	91%	88%	43%	89%	89%	40%
Household size*	2.1 (1.1)	3.4 (1.7)	3.2 (1.8)	2.5 (1.4)	3.5 (1.6)	3.4 (1.8)	2.6 (1.6)	3.7 (1.7)	3.5 (1.7)
Highest education									
Primary dropout	12%	3%	0%	12%	2%	0%	14%	4%	1%
Primary	79%	28%	6%	84%	44%	13%	72%	57%	17%
Lower secondary	5%	24%	21%	3%	17%	12%	5%	10%	13%
Higher secondary	3%	34%	49%	1%	19%	32%	5%	17%	33%
Lower tertiary or above	1%	11%	23%	0%	18%	43%	5%	13%	37%
Average education*	2.0 (0.6)	3.2 (1.1)	3.9 (0.8)	1.9 (0.4)	3.1 (1.2)	4.0 (1.0)	2.2 (0.9)	2.8 (1.2)	3.9 (1.1)
Non-financial asset holdings *	0.9 (1.2)	1.2 (1.4)	0.6 (1.2)	3.4 (1.3)	2.4 (1.8)	1.5 (1.7)	3.1 (1.3)	2.0 (1.6)	1.3 (1.5)

Note: * Mean scores. Standard deviations in parenthesis.
Source: 2000 Families Survey, personal data

by Germany, Belgium, the Netherlands, Sweden and Denmark in ascending order. Across all generations, the settlers exhibit the highest levels of monetary poverty as compared with their returnee and stayer counterparts. With 79 per cent, the first generation of settlers appears as the most impoverished. The settlers from the second and third generations fare relatively better than their first-generation counterparts but nearly half of them continue to live in poverty. In the case of the returnees and the stayers, members of the second generation turned out to be the poorest. At 51 per cent, the settlers display a greater tendency than the returnees and stayers to have poor-income parents, while the parents of the returnees and the stayers tend to be impoverished to a similar extent.

Results from the three-way comparisons

Tables 5.4, 5.5 and 5.6 display the results obtained from the probit models, comparing the three groups aggregately as well as separately. Model 1 presented in Table 5.4 confirms the tendencies emerging from the frequency distributions by demonstrating that the settlers across all EU destinations experience monetary poverty to a significantly greater extent than the stayers as well as the returnees who comprise the least impoverished group. As can be seen from Table 5.5 demonstrating the results obtained from the separate analyses, the observed differences persist across generations. While Model 1 indicates a greater propensity for the first generation to experience monetary poverty than the subsequent ones, it is evident from Table 5.5 that the probability of falling into monetary poverty is considerably higher for the first generation of settlers than their stayer counterparts. Table 5.5 also shows that the probability does not vary between the settlers from the second and third generations while it declines substantially for the stayers as they move from the second to the third generation. From Model 1, it may appear that having a migrant ancestor matters very little; however, the separate analyses do

Table 5.4: Pooled probit models of monetary poverty

	Model 1	Model 2 – dyadic
Migrant ancestry (a)	–0.09 (0.07)	–0.08 (0.09)
Individual migration status in context (b)		
Returnees to Turkey	**–0.20 (0.08)** *	0.02 (0.14)
Settlers in Germany	**0.50 (0.09)** ***	0.40 (0.11) ***
The Netherlands	**0.62 (0.13)** ***	0.37 (0.20)
France	**0.38 (0.15)** *	–0.01 (0.24)
Austria	**0.96 (0.19)** ***	0.98 (0.20) ***
Belgium	**0.69 (0.09)** ***	0.57 (0.12) ***
Denmark	**0.91 (0.16)** ***	0.87 (0.24) ***
Sweden	**0.91 (0.14)** ***	0.92 (0.21) ***
Other EU country	**0.78 (0.25)** **	0.72 (0.23) **
Family generations (c)		
G1	**0.51 (0.12)** ***	Not applicable
G3	–0.14 (0.08)	–0.15 (0.10)
Parental monetary poverty (d)	Not applicable	**0.62 (0.07)** ***
Age	–0.01 (0.00)	–0.01 (0.01)
Sex (e)	**–0.10 (0.05)** *	–0.18 (0.07) **
Marital status (f)	–0.06 (0.06)	–0.13 (0.09)
Household size	**0.22 (0.02)** ***	0.23 (0.02) ***
Highest education (g)		
Primary dropout	0.11 (0.13)	0.26 (0.28)
Lower secondary	**–0.35 (0.08)** ***	–0.45 (0.11) ***
Higher secondary	**–0.50 (0.07)** ***	–0.53 (0.10) ***
Lower tertiary or above	**–0.66 (0.08)** ***	–0.66 (0.10) ***
Non-financial asset holdings	**–0.08 (0.02)** ***	–0.08 (0.02) **
Intercept	–0.47 (0.18) *	–0.52 (0.26) *

Table 5.4: Pooled probit models of monetary poverty (continued)

	Model 1	Model 2 – dyadic
Observations	3,761	1,889
Pseudo R^2	0.12	0.16

Notes: Standard errors in parentheses. * $p < 0.05$, ** $p < 0.01$, *** $p < 0.001$
(**a**) baseline: families with non-migrant ancestors;
(**b**) baseline: stayers in Turkey (**c**) baseline: G2 – second generation;
(**d**) baseline: non-poor parents; (**e**) baseline: women;
(**f**) baseline: unmarried; (**g**) baseline: primary.
Source: 2000 Families Survey, personal data

indicate reduced likelihood of monetary poverty for the settlers and the returnees with migrant ancestry.

Model 2 presented in Table 5.4 demonstrates that adult children with monetarily impoverished parents are more likely to fall into the same poverty trap than those with non-poor parents. The results obtained from the separate dyadic analyses, however, reveal significant group differences in the extent to which monetary poverty is transmitted across family generations. As can be seen from Table 5.6, while the probability of *direct* transmission from parents to their *own* children proved insignificant for the returnees, it remains strong among the other two groups. The likelihood of transmission turned out to be slightly higher for the stayers than the settlers.

Turning to summarise the outcomes concerning key confounders, Model 1 suggests no significant association between age and monetary poverty (Table 5.4), but the latter seems to decline with age in the case of the stayers only (Table 5.5). Regarding sex, Model 1 reveals a significantly lower tendency for women than men to fall into monetary poverty, but as is evident from Table 5.5, the observed gender differences are significant only for the stayers. As for household size, Model 1 shows that the larger the household, the greater the likelihood of experiencing monetary poverty (Table 5.4), but this tendency does not apply to the stayers (Table 5.5).

Table 5.5: Separate probit models of monetary poverty

	Settlers in Europe	Returnees to Turkey	Stayers in Turkey
Migrant ancestry (a)	**–0.35 (0.16)** *	**–0.61 (0.27)** *	–0.03 (0.08)
Family generations (b)			
G1	**0.74 (0.20)** ***	–0.18 (0.29)	**0.48 (0.21)** *
G3	0.11 (0.13)	0.24 (0.29)	**–0.33 (0.11)** **
Age	0.01 (0.01)	0.01 (0.01)	**–0.02 (0.01)** **
Sex (c)	–0.05 (0.08)	–0.02 (0.19)	**–0.15 (0.07)** *
Marital status (d)	–0.18 (0.10)	0.16 (0.20)	–0.03 (0.09)
Household size	**0.25 (0.03)** ***	**0.25 (0.04)** ***	0.20 (0.22)
Highest education (e)			
Primary dropout	0.06 (0.24)	0.12 (0.24)	0.21 (0.20)
Lower secondary	**–0.40 (0.11)** ***	–0.22 (0.23)	–0.17 (0.12)
Higher secondary	**–0.33 (0.11)** **	0.14 (0.23)	**–0.64 (0.09)** ***
Lower tertiary or above	**–0.45 (0.14)** **	**–0.92 (0.28)** **	**–0.68 (0.10)** ***
Non-financial asset holdings	**–0.16 (0.03)** ***	0.02 (0.04)	–0.03 (0.02)
Constant	–0.31 (0.32)	–1.30 (0.56) *	0.01 (0.24)
Observations	1377	587	1783
Pseudo R^2	0.12	0.11	0.10

Notes: Standard errors in parentheses. $^{*}p < 0.05$, $^{**}p < 0.01$, $^{***}p < 0.001$
(a) baseline: families with non-migrant ancestors; **(b)** baseline: G2 – second generation; **(c)** baseline: women; **(d)** baseline: unmarried; **(e)** baseline: primary.

Source: 2000 Families Survey, personal data

Table 5.6: Separate probit models of monetary poverty – dyadic

	Settlers in Europe	Returnees to Turkey	Stayers in Turkey
Migrant ancestry (a)	–0.28 (0.21)	–1.52 (0.57) **	–0.01 (0.11)
Family generations (b)			
G1	Not applicable	Not applicable	Not applicable
G3	0.13 (0.16)	–0.01 (0.40)	–0.37 (0.14) *
Parental monetary poverty (c)	**0.54 (012) *****	**0.41 (0.31)**	**0.74 (0.09) *****
Age	–0.00 (0.01)	0.02 (0.02)	–0.01 (0.01)
Sex (d)	–0.03 (0.11)	–0.09 (0.28)	–0.26 (0.09) **
Marital status (e)	–0.23 (0.4)	–0.01 (0.40)	–0.07 (0.12)
Household size	0.29 (0.04) ***	0.39 (0.12) **	0.17 (0.03) ***
Highest education (f)			
Primary dropout	0.13 (0.53)	Not applicable	0.22 (0.32)
Lower secondary	–0.63 (0.17) ***	–0.53 (0.36)	–0.25 (0.15)
Higher secondary	–0.50 (0.17) **	–0.20 (0.37)	–0.56 (0.13) ***
Lower tertiary or above	–0.63 (0.20) **	–0.77 (0.40)	–0.59 (0.12) ***
Non-financial asset holdings	**–0.13 (0.05) ****	–0.13 (0.08)	**–0.06 (0.03) ***
Constant	–0.36 (0.45)	–1.06 (1.14)	–0.22 (0.33)
Observations	701	122	1059
Pseudo R^2	0.14	0.19	0.14

Notes: Standard errors in parentheses. * $p < 0.05$, ** $p < 0.01$, *** $p < 0.001$
(a) baseline: families with non-migrant ancestors; **(b)** baseline: G2 – second generation; **(c)** baseline: non-poor parents **(d)** baseline: women; **(e)** baseline: unmarried; **(f)** baseline: primary.

Source: 2000 Families Survey, personal data

While Model 1 suggests a decline in monetary poverty with increased educational attainment (Table 5.4), nuanced group differences emerge from the separate analyses (Table 5.5). For the settlers, the likelihood of suffering from poverty is lower for those educated at the levels of lower secondary or lower tertiary and above than their counterparts with a primary school diploma. Of the returnees, only those with lower tertiary education and above display a significantly lower tendency to become monetarily impoverished. As for the stayers, the propensity is substantially reduced for those with higher secondary and tertiary education. Across the three groups, the poverty-reducing effect of tertiary education appears to be the greatest for the returnees. Strikingly, the probability of falling into monetary poverty turned out to be lower for the stayers with higher secondary and tertiary education than the settlers educated to the same level, while the reverse remains true for those with lower secondary education.

Finally, Model 1 indicates a considerably lower propensity for those with more non-financial asset accumulations to experience monetary poverty (Table 5.4). However, this tendency appears significant only in the case of the settlers (Table 5.5), confirming the cash-generating capacity of their house, land and/or business-related assets. Having said this, the auxiliary analyses suggest no substantial variation between the settlers who are/were self-employed in a private business and their counterparts who work(ed) as a public or private sector employee in their current or last job (probit = 0.06, p = 0.67, N = 1,103). The same applies to the returnees (probit = 0.05, p = 0.74, N = 520), whereas the poverty risk appears to be considerably greater for the self-employed stayers (probit = 0.25, $p < 0.05$, N = 1,118).

Results from the sub-analyses

Table 5.7 presents the probit results obtained from the sub-analyses of monetary poverty among the settlers. Three models are estimated here: Model A to assess the statistical significance of the destination country differences observed in the settlers' monetary poverty levels (see Table 5.2); Model B to examine the poverty impact of the welfare generosity and effort exerted by the receiving country governments without falling into ecological fallacy; and Model C to check whether the findings presented earlier about the strength of intergenerational transmission of poverty among the settlers still hold.

The results emerging from Models A and B are mostly confirmatory of each other, except for those concerning migrant ancestry. While Model A suggests that migrant ancestry makes no significant difference to monetary poverty, Model B detects a significant, inverse correlation between the two, meaning that having a migrant ancestor in the family may have a poverty-reducing effect. Having said this, it is the first generation of settlers who prove to be significantly more likely than their second-generation counterparts to fall into monetary poverty. No notable differences are observed between the members of the second and third generations, but as shown by Model C, the likelihood of falling into monetary poverty remains to be substantially greater for the settlers with monetarily impoverished parents.

The portion of lifetime the settlers spent in Europe, however, appears not to matter. Model A reveals that the settlers in Austria, Belgium, Denmark and Sweden fare significantly worse than their counterparts in Germany, while the differences observed in the poverty levels for those residing in Germany, France and the Netherlands prove to be statistically insignificant. Rather counter-intuitively, Model B, performed to make sense of the observed country variations, shows that the settlers living under more generous welfare regimes are significantly more likely to experience monetary poverty. This pattern, however, does not apply to the settlers in Austria, combining the highest level of monetary poverty with a relatively low welfare effort score (that is, 6.34). To further explain the differences in the poverty levels observed for the settlers, separate auxiliary

Table 5.7: Sub-group analyses: probit estimations of monetary poverty among settlers

	Model A	Model B	Model C – dyadic
Migrant ancestry (a)	–0.32 (0.18)	**–0.35 (0.18)** *	–0.33 (0.23)
Family generations (b)			
G1	**0.86 (0.22)** ***	**0.81 (0.22)** ***	Not applicable
G3	0.10 (0.14)	0.14 (0.14)	0.19 (0.18)
Lifetime in Europe	–0.08 (0.25)	–0.19 (0.24)	–0.06 (0.31)
Destination country (c)			
The Netherlands	0.21 (0.16)	Not applicable	Not applicable
France	0.07 (0.18)	Not applicable	Not applicable
Austria	**0.50 (0.23)** *	Not applicable	Not applicable
Belgium	**0.46 (0.14)** **	Not applicable	Not applicable
Denmark	**0.50 (0.20)** *	Not applicable	Not applicable
Sweden	**0.62 (0.19)** **	Not applicable	Not applicable
Other EU country	0.42 (0.29)	Not applicable	Not applicable
Welfare generosity	Not applicable	**0.09 (0.03)** **	**0.10 (0.04)** *

Table 5.7: Sub-group analyses: probit estimations of monetary poverty among settlers (continued)

	Model A	**Model B**	**Model C – dyadic**
Destination country citizenship (d)			
Native-born citizen	–0.13 (0.14)	–0.07 (0.14)	–0.30 (0.16)
Naturalised citizen	**–0.33 (0.11)** **	**–0.28 (0.10)** **	**–0.52 (0.16)** **
Parental monetary poverty	Not applicable	Not applicable	**0.53 (0.13)** ***
Age	0.01 (0.01)	0.01 (0.01)	0.00 (0.01)
Sex (e)	–0.04 (0.09)	–0.06 (0.09)	–0.05 (0.12)
Ethnicity (f)			
Kurdish	0.17 (0.12)	0.24 (0.14)	0.13 (0.19)
Other	–0.00 (0.16)	–0.03 (0.15)	0.09 (0.22)
Marital status (g)	**–0.26 (0.12)** *	**–0.23 (0.12)** *	–0.25 (0.16)
Household size	**0.27 (0.03)** ***	**0.26 (0.32)** ***	**0.31 (0.04)** ***

(continued)

Table 5.7: Sub-group analyses: probit estimations of monetary poverty among settlers (continued)

	Model A	**Model B**	**Model C – dyadic**
Highest education (h)			
Primary dropout	0.16 (0.25)	0.15 (0.25)	0.20 (0.54)
Lower secondary	**–0.32 (0.13)** *	**–0.34 (0.13)** *	**–0.57 (0.20)** **
Higher secondary	–0.21 (0.3)	**–0.24 (0.12)** *	**–0.39 (0.19)** *
Lower tertiary or above	**–0.38 (0.16)** *	**–0.41 (0.16)** *	**–0.57 (0.23)** *
Non-financial asset holdings in Europe	**–0.12 (0.04)** *	**–0.11 (0.03)** **	–0.06 (0.05)
Non-financial asset holdings in Turkey	–0.03 (0.03)	–0.02 (0.03)	–0.09 (0.05)
Inter-ethnic friendship ties	0.02 (0.03)	0.03 (0.03)	0.01 (0.05)
Intercept	–0.82 (0.41) *	–1.51 (0.46) **	–1.27 (0.66) *
Observations	1196	1196	602
Pseudo R^2	0.15	0.14	0.17

Notes: Standard errors in parentheses. * $p < 0.05$, ** $p < 0.01$, *** $p < 0.001$

(a) baseline: non-migrant ancestry; **(b)** baseline: G2 – second generation; **(c)** baseline: Germany; **(d)** baseline: non-citizen; **(e)** baseline: women; **(f)** baseline: Turkish; **(g)** baseline: unmarried; **(h)** baseline: primary graduate; **(i)** baseline: non-poor parents

Source: 2000 Families Survey, personal data

analyses were performed through including labour market mobility and anti-discrimination variables within Model B; however, neither of these variables proved to be significantly associated with monetary poverty (probit for labour market mobility = −0.01, se = 0.00, p = 0.144, and probit for anti-discrimination = −0.01, se = 0.00, p = 0.057). The insignificant results indicate that the settlers living in destination countries whose governments are considered to adopt more favourable policies in terms of promoting labour market mobility and fighting discrimination on the basis of an equal opportunities principle are not necessarily better off.

Holding destination country citizenship does seem to make a positive difference to migrant poverty but only in the case of the naturalised citizens. While this group of settlers are found to be considerably less likely to fall into monetary poverty than their non-citizen counterparts, no significant difference is observed between native-born citizens and non-citizens. Besides, the auxiliary analyses performed using naturalised citizens as the reference category show that the likelihood of experiencing monetary poverty does not vary significantly between the naturalised and native-born citizens (probit = 0.09, se = 0.14, p = 0.485).

Turning to sum up the outcomes concerning the key confounders, monetary poverty turned out not to be correlated significantly with age, gender or ethnic identity but with marital status and household size. The likelihood of falling into monetary poverty is documented to be substantially greater for unmarried settlers and those living in larger households. This tendency has, however, little to do with the share of minors (that is, children aged below 18) given the results from the auxiliary analyses, indicating reduced monetary poverty among households where a greater proportion of their membership is made up of minors (probit = −0.19, se = 0.08, $p < 0.05$).

The relationship between education and monetary poverty proved to be more complex. None of the models indicate a steady decline in monetary poverty with upward movement in the educational ladder. While a modest improvement is observed in the poverty status of those with lower secondary and tertiary education, higher secondary graduates appear not to fare as well.

The non-financial investments the settlers made in Europe are found to be inversely associated with monetary poverty. The same cannot, however, be said about the equivalent assets they had accumulated in Turkey. Having more inter-ethnic ties within their friendship circles does not seem to make a significant difference to their impoverishment, either.

The story: an interpretation of the results

This section returns to the main quest of the book, that is, to question whether migration to Europe has been economically beneficial for the migrants and their descendants who originated from Turkey, and to address this question in light of the emerging research evidence on monetary poverty. Monetary poverty is not the sole criterion one can use to assess economic (dis)benefits, but due to it being a key indicator of welfare and material wellbeing, it remains of paramount importance to establish how far, and in what ways, the migration journey contributed to its reduction.

Some 60 years ago, the bilateral agreements signed off between Turkey and many Northern and Western European countries granted people from Turkey an opportunity to become guest-workers in these countries' mining, manufacturing and construction industries. Some, mostly men, took up this opportunity while others did not, or could not, for example, due to failing the recruitment tests (see, for example, Berger and Mohr 1975/2010 for vivid imagery of the tests the candidates underwent). There exists no statistical evidence to determine how poor the movers were at the time of migration. However, given the economically driven nature of the guest-worker movement, it is highly probable that they were then poorer than those who did not leave their origins.

It is indeed anecdotally known that the male ancestors who moved from the selected regions of Turkey during guest-worker years tended to be landless poor unable to store food for winter. More often than not, they left their origins not for adventure but with the hope of escaping poverty. They went to Europe initially as sojourners with no intention to settle there. Their plan was to come back after having made enough money, for example, to buy agricultural land, equipment or livestock – but not all went according to plan. Many of them ended up settling there with their families. Some did return to Turkey to reunite with the wives and children they had left behind, or to start anew, while others moved back with or without their descendants in Europe.

Not only the first generation of returnees but also the subsequent ones appear as the greatest beneficiaries of their migration journey, given their propensity to experience poverty to the least extent. The highly educated returnees fare significantly better than their counterparts with a primary school diploma most likely because the Turkish labour market presents them with an opportunity to cash in the formal cultural capital they have accrued during their time abroad. Poverty experiences of the returnees with less than university or equivalent education do not seem to differ substantially, however. Despite most of them being primary school graduates, this group of returnees still manage to remain above the threshold to a greater extent than the stayers and the settlers alike. They must owe this partly to migration and the power of migrant money. As also documented in Eroğlu (2021), the returnees, on average, own the highest stock of non-financial (that is, house, land and/or business-related) assets in Turkey – the country where they currently reside. Contrary to expectations, the returnees' non-financial asset accumulations appear to make little contribution to reducing the risk of falling into monetary poverty; however, their contribution is likely to have been underestimated, as the poverty measure used here is neither sensitive to the housing costs nor to the use values of their non-financial assets (for example, rent-free living in owner-occupied accommodation). Having said this, it remains probable that their holdings are rather limited in their capacity to generate cash. Though it is not demonstrated here empirically, the returnees may also be generating rent from the financial investments (for example, savings) they have made during their stay in Europe. Besides, given the inverse relationship observed between migrant ancestry and monetary poverty, it is highly likely that wealth is trickling down to the returnees from their male migrant ancestors in some monetary form. The returnees are indeed unique in terms of their success in breaking the transmission of poverty from parents to children, and not only their own migration decisions but also those of their male ancestors seem to have contributed substantially to this outcome.

The stayers, on the other hand, do not fare as well as the returnees. While it cannot be empirically established here, they may well have fallen behind the returnees by 'deciding' to stay. They cannot, however, be said to have done too badly, especially when compared with the settlers in Europe. Not only do the stayers across all three generations become less exposed to the risk of monetary poverty than their settler counterparts, but also the risk declines appreciably by the third generation. This generational trend seems to be driven more by increased educational attainment than non-financial asset accumulation. Indeed, the stayers' educational attainment levels improve considerably as they move down the generational line. However, their relative advantage cannot simply be explained through increased educational attainment, considering that, on average, the settlers achieve similar or higher levels of education than the stayers across the three generations.

The sources of their (dis)advantage seem to lie more in the welfare systems and the labour markets in which they currently operate. The stayers from the first generation have most likely been able to secure more favourable state pensions and retirement conditions than their settler counterparts, or live in extended families that are monetarily non-poor. As for the working stayers, the Turkish labour market is not a bed of roses; therefore, they are highly likely to encounter adversities there in the form of unemployment, low pay, occupational hazards and so on. However, the working stayers seem to be acquiring higher returns on their educational qualifications than their settler counterparts, raising more of them above the poverty line. It is therefore probable that the stayers are experiencing less of a blockage than the settlers in access to jobs that are commensurate with their educational achievements. Having said this, regardless of their position in the family genealogy, female stayers tend to be more impoverished than their male counterparts. This could well mean that women in Turkey are facing greater blockages than men in access to educational and labour market opportunities.

Contrary to education, the stayers' non-financial investments appear to make little difference to their impoverished predicament. This is rather surprising, considering their propensity to accumulate more than the settlers (see also Eroğlu 2021). However, like the returnees, they might well have invested in non-financial assets that are rather restricted in their cash-generating capacity. For reasons explained earlier, this should, however, not be taken to mean that their non-financial investments do not matter at all. The stayers are, indeed, more likely than the settlers to own a house and hence enjoy rent-free accommodation (Eroğlu 2021). Thus, their non-financial assets must be helping them to reduce monetary poverty, but rather indirectly.

When it comes to the intergenerational transmission of poverty, the stayers do not prove as advantaged, however. Unlike the returnees, they continue to transmit monetary poverty to a significant and slightly higher extent than the settlers. The persistence of strong transmission from parents to children can be attributed to the absence of a well-developed welfare system that protects the stayers, for example, from the adverse influences operating within the Turkish labour market.

Turning to the group that emerges as the worst off – that is, the settlers. Across all destinations and generations, they suffer from monetary poverty to a considerably greater extent than those who stayed in Turkey and who returned to their origins. The picture looks particularly bleak for the male ancestors. These men, on average, arrived in Europe in their late 20s (mean age at arrival = 29, sd = 6) as guest-workers and had spent 42 years of their lives there (sd = 4), reaching a pensionable age (mean age = 71, sd = 5). Their migration to Europe might well have had a poverty-reducing effect by enabling them to find manual work and make money in the buoyant European labour markets of the time. Any such improvement cannot, however, be empirically documented here due to an absence of information about their pre-migration poverty status. However, it is clear from the emerging evidence that the great majority of these men are monetarily impoverished in old age. They may or may not be a pension recipient, but even if they are, their pensions are clearly not enough to lift them above the income threshold. These men made a substantial contribution to the reconstruction of Europe with their manual labour, and it appears that they have been used and cast aside. Contrary to the assimilationist expectations, having spent a large portion of their lives in Europe seems to have helped them very little in terms of escaping poverty in old age.

Relative to their first-generation counterparts, the settlers from the second and third generations fare better. However, nearly half of them still find themselves in monetary poverty and in a less favourable position than their returnee and stayer counterparts. The settlers' impoverishment does not lessen as they move down from the second to the third generation. While they transmit monetary poverty to a slightly lesser extent than the stayers, the likelihood of transmission remains strong for both groups.

Income sharing across generations may be partly responsible for the observed (inter)generational tendencies, but there is more to these trends than initially meets the eye. At face value, the improvement from the first to the second generation appears supportive of the assimilationist expectations; however, it cannot readily be taken to mean that younger generations are successfully integrating into the European labour markets. Here is why.

The observed generational trends are occurring fundamentally because the first-generation settlers have moved into the retirement phase of their life course under highly unfavourable conditions – *not* because subsequent generations have become increasingly more able to attain prestigious, well-paid jobs that are commensurate with their educational qualifications. Clearly, not all settlers are low achievers educationally. Particularly members of the second and third generations tend to be better educated, and yet, except for those with lower secondary education, the settlers exhibit less of a chance to move out of monetary poverty than their stayer counterparts with the same level of education. Their chances do not improve steadily with increased education either. It hence remains highly likely that the settlers are experiencing diminishing returns from their educational achievements. This possibility is further supported by the modest correlation observed between occupational prestige (ISEI scores) and highest qualification achieved ($r = 0.398$, $p < 0.001$), indicating a mismatch between educational and occupational attainment.

Moreover, as shown previously by the author (Eroğlu 2018), having been denied salaried job opportunities, the settlers, including those with university and equivalent degrees, are venturing mostly into low-status, small businesses in retail, wholesale and hospitality sectors in considerable numbers. This tendency is particularly applicable to the settlers from subsequent generations. During the guest-worker years, manual work was in abundance; therefore, the first-generation men did not encounter much difficulty in finding employment. However, the younger generations have become more exposed to unemployment and blocked opportunities in the salaried parts of the labour market after the economic crisis in the

1970s, and have hence been increasingly compelled to venture into small businesses (Eroğlu 2018). Through engagement in such businesses, particularly members of the second generation appear to have generated more non-financial assets in Europe than their first-generation counterparts who, possibly due to their initial sojourner status as guest-workers, directed their investments more towards Turkey (non-financial asset holdings in Europe: G1 mean = 1, sd = 1.2; G2 mean = 1.3, sd = 1.5; G3 mean = 0.7, sd = 1.2; and for non-financial asset holdings in Turkey: G1 mean = 3, sd = 1.4; G2 mean = 1.4, sd = 1.5; G3 mean = 0.8, sd = 1.3). This possibility is further supported by the observed generational propensities for business-related asset ownership among the settlers (conditional distributions for business-related assets owned in Europe: G1 = 5 per cent, G2 = 14 per cent, G3 = 7 per cent and in Turkey: G1 = 7 per cent, G2 = 5 per cent, G3 = 4 per cent).

The generational move towards self-employment is congruous with the positive association observed between the settlers' monetary poverty levels and their non-financial investments in Europe. It is also understandable why their equivalent holdings in Turkey might be contributing very little to poverty reduction. The first-generation settlers most likely purchased house and/or land type assets in their rural origins that are low in value, or have limited cash-generating capacity, or both. They may also be unable to generate revenue from some of their assets due to their being designated for free use of their close relatives in Turkey. Moreover, any value or revenue they acquire from their non-financial assets in Turkey is likely to disappear into thin air when converted into a European country currency. Having said this, like their stayer counterparts, a sub-group of the settlers from younger generations seems to have made some non-financial investments in Turkey, making a marginal contribution to reducing the risk of monetary poverty.

Clearly, the settlers' escape route out of poverty is not straightforward and typical of what one would expect to see in labour markets that claim to be operating on the basis of meritocratic principles. Gaining more education does not necessarily give them the opportunity to attain better-paid, more prestigious jobs in the salaried parts of the labour market. Being faced with blocked opportunities in this part of the labour market, particularly the younger generations are turning to self-employment, although it does not *necessarily* give them a better chance of exiting monetary poverty than salaried employment. Hence, it is not surprising to see that the settlers have achieved very little success in terms of preventing the transmission of poverty on to younger generations.

The settlers' poverty trajectories appear not to be as gendered as the stayers, however. Settler women tend to be as impoverished as their male counterparts and vice versa. This might be attributable to the chosen poverty measure being based on household income. However, the sensitivity of the measure to pick up gender differences among the stayers strengthens the possibility of a migration effect. Migration to Europe may well be making a positive difference by exposing the settlers to less patriarchal contexts where women are actively encouraged to participate in economic and social life. This possibility is reinforced by the greater propensity for the settler women to take up employment (56 per cent) than their returnee (7 per cent) and stayer counterparts (37 per cent). One might explain the observed differences in women's employment through self-selection, suggesting that migrants may well have been more progressive in their gender-related attitudes prior to migration. However, since the sampled migrants originate from rural, conservative parts of Turkey, such positive self-selection is rather unlikely. Migration may have also physically distanced some of the settlers from their families, leading to reduced parental control. This may have, in turn, given the (female) children freedom to make more progressive decisions about their work, family and social lives. However, such an affirmative influence of migration should not disguise the fact that it only makes a marginal difference to monetary poverty and its transmission across settler generations, most likely due to unfavourable pay and working conditions affecting both men and women.

The settlers also appear to be benefitting from the migration decisions of their male ancestors to a degree. However, given the propensity of the first-generation settlers to suffer more from monetary poverty and own fewer assets in Europe (see above for average scores), having migrant ancestry is less likely to be reducing the younger generations' exposure to poverty risk through direct transfer of money or economic capital. It may rather be helping through mobilisation of other resource types, for example, social and informal cultural capital. This way, migration might be making a faint contribution to lessening the intergenerational transmission of poverty among the settlers.

Regardless of their generational position, the settlers living in larger households fare worse than those living in smaller households. This group of settlers are exposed to the increased risk of monetary poverty not because they have a disproportionately greater share of minors that are unable to join the family labour force. On the contrary, the risk appears to be lower for households with more minors, and they may well owe this to living under continental welfare regimes that offer some protection for families with children. Households consisting of more adults, however, seem less protected. Unfortunately, it is not possible to represent here the diversity in the composition of the larger households, and demonstrate how it correlates with poverty, but they include a mix of workers, carers, university students, the frail elderly, the disabled and the unemployed. Many of these groups would need state protection but do not necessarily benefit from the generosity of welfare states.

Ironically, the most impoverished settlers turned out to be living under more generous welfare regimes. Those based in Austria, Belgium, Denmark and Sweden proved significantly more impoverished than their counterparts in Germany, and with the exception of Austria, these countries possess some of the most generous welfare systems in the world. Living under a less generous welfare regime is likely to contribute to the increased level of monetary poverty experienced by the settlers in Austria but there seems to be more to the story. The predicament of the settlers in Belgium, Denmark and Sweden suggests that they may well be denied the generosity of the welfare states when it comes to pensions or other cash benefits. The settlers in Belgium exhibit the highest level of unemployment at 7.4 per cent, which stood marginally above the 2011 rate for the general population – that is, 7.2 per cent (OECD 2011). It is hence possible that this group of settlers are not adequately supported by the Belgian welfare state in the aftermath of the financial crisis, which appears to have hit the country's labour market harder than any other destination studied. As a matter of fact, with 2 per cent, the unemployment rate was considerably lower for the settlers in Sweden than it was for those based not only in Belgium but also Austria (4.5 per cent), Denmark (5.3 per cent), Germany (5.8 per cent), France (3 per cent) and the Netherlands (4.6 per cent). It is clear from the evidence that the settlers in Denmark and Sweden are neither affected by unemployment as hard as their counterparts in Belgium nor excluded from paid work opportunities to a greater extent than those based in Germany, and yet they suffer from higher levels of monetary poverty.

In addition to having access to limited welfare, or being denied welfare generosity, a further explanation can be provided for this intriguing picture, taking into account the labour market participation rates, which proved to be the highest for the settlers in Austria (57.3 per cent), Denmark (57.2 per cent) and Sweden (61 per cent). Coupled with the observed poverty ratios, the results are indicative of in-work poverty. Indeed, these countries occupy the top three places in their share of monetarily poor settlers who are currently in paid work. The respective figures are 46 per cent, 50 per cent and 55 per cent for Austria, Denmark and Sweden. Evidently, the settlers based in these countries are becoming integrated into the lower echelons of the labour market at a higher rate than their counterparts living in other destinations studied. The incidence of the aforementioned mismatch between educational and occupational attainment is also likely to be greater, especially in Denmark and Sweden where the settlers' average level of education remains at or above the average for the settlers in Europe (Austria = 3.1, sd = 1.02; Denmark = 3.3, sd = 1.2; Sweden = 3.5, sd = 1.1; Europe = 3.3, sd = 1.1).

Hence, it is probable that more of the settlers in these countries might be settling for low-paid jobs not simply because they are low achievers educationally but also because they are being blocked from better-paid job opportunities. This may come as a surprise considering that the Swedish government policies achieved the top scores on both MIPEX anti-discrimination and labour market mobility indices, yet remains congruent with the probit results obtained from the auxiliary analyses, which show that the settlers living in destination countries with more favourable policies in terms of enabling access to the labour market and fighting discrimination, based on the equal opportunities principle do not necessarily fare better. Thus, the failures of the destination countries to tackle migrant poverty cannot simply be attributed to the unfavourability or inadequacy of the policies adopted. There also seem to be structural impediments to achieving 'real' equality of opportunity, and these include the systemic racism and discriminatory practices continuing to operate at the ground level without being detected or challenged.

Destination country citizenship, however, seems to offer some protection for the settlers against the risk of monetary poverty. While naturalised and native-born citizens are exposed to the risk to a similar extent, the former does significantly better than the non-citizens. The same is, however, untrue for the native-born. One might explain this through motivation. Coming from abroad with the intention to make money, the naturalised citizens might be more motivated to convert their legal entitlements into cash. Despite possessing the same entitlements, the native-born citizens might not be as economically driven. However, motivational differences can only explain a small part of the story. Given the within- and between-country variations in the rights and conditions of access to work and welfare granted to legal residents and citizens, coupled with the advantages the native-born would be expected to possess due to having undergone the same schooling system as the majority, and speaking the country language more like a 'native', the native-born citizens should have done better than the non-citizens. But rather curiously, they do not.

Perhaps the answer to this conundrum partly lies in their lack of acceptance by the public as 'one of their own'. Another explanation seems to lie in the immigration policies and systems put in place by the receiving country governments. Looking at the composition of the non-citizens, one can see that 21 per cent (188 out of 918) of the native-born settlers lack destination country citizenship. Of these, 65 per cent currently reside in Germany where the migrants' native-born children are not granted citizenship by birth. However, the question remains as to why they do not apply for it in adulthood. One possible explanation is to do with the denial of rights to dual citizenship by the receiving country government(s) while Turkey allows for it. The imposition of a forced choice between their country of origin and destination might be a big deal for the settlers, considering their tendency to exhibit strong attachments to Turkey. This tendency remains strong even for the native-born, who make up 40 per cent of the settlers (925 out of 2,318) and 74 per cent of the third generation (663 out of 900), given the evidence that 98 per cent of the native-born want to be buried in Turkey and more than 90 per cent of them support Turkey in Eurovision song contests or football matches between Turkey and the destination country. By denying them the legal protection against the poverty risk that comes with citizenship, destination countries, like Germany, which prohibits dual citizenship, seem to be penalising those with particularly strong attachments to Turkey.

Consequently, while systemic/institutional racism has not been directly observed here, the emerging evidence provides substantial support for its continued existence in the lives of the settlers as a factor that prevents them from making progress. Even those who spent most or the whole of their lifetime in Europe do not necessary fare better, which is clearly an indication of the receiving societies' and their institutions' negativity or indifference towards the settlers and their predicament. Holders of destination country citizenship might be better shielded against systemic racism, but even the native-born do not necessarily benefit from such legal protection. Coupled with adverse (labour) market conditions and limited access to welfare, the discriminatory practices that result from systemic/institutional racism are bound to play a major part in inflicting monetary poverty and allowing it to persist across generations.

Conclusion

The migration journey of the returnees from all three generations seems to have helped them escape poverty to a considerable extent. The picture, however, appears less rosy for the settlers in Europe. This group of migrants might be less poor now than they would have been had they remained in Turkey; so, to a degree, they might have still benefitted from their (ancestors') decision to leave their origins. However, the fact remains that the settlers are the most monetarily impoverished across all generations and destinations in Europe. One day, if they return to Turkey, they may well benefit from the power of migrant money, but where they are based currently, they stand less of a chance of escaping monetary poverty and preventing its transmission onto younger generations than their counterparts who returned to their origins.

SIX

Conclusion

This chapter provides a summary of the key findings, along with a discussion of their implications for research, theory and policy making. It then turns to address the research limitations and concludes with an agenda for future research.

Key findings and implications for policy

This study sought to explore the poverty consequences of international migration from a unique multi-site and intergenerational perspective, based on comparisons across three family generations of settler and returnee migrants and their stayer counterparts who remained in their country of origin.

The emerging evidence confirms Hypothesis 1, which expects the settlers to fare the worst. The first generation of settlers, who contributed to the construction of post-war Europe, are exposed to the highest risk of poverty at their pensionable age, followed by their younger counterparts. Hence, migration to Europe cannot be said to have been as economically beneficial for the settlers as it has been for the returnees who across all generations fare the best. The settlers from subsequent generations do, nevertheless, accrue some economic benefits from their ancestors' decisions to migrate. These benefits seem to trickle down not so much through direct transfer of economic capital (that is, money or assets) but possibly through conversion of their male ancestors' social and informal cultural capital accumulations (connections, knowledge and experience) into cash. The migration journey seems to have helped female settlers to a degree by giving them the chance to live and work in less patriarchal contexts. However, in line with Hypothesis 2 and Hooijer and Picot's (2015) findings, the settlers remain excluded from the opportunity to enjoy the benefits of welfare states renowned for their generosity.

At first sight, the evidence may appear to provide only partial support for Hypothesis 3, which predicts little improvement in the poverty status of the settlers across generations. However, although the risk of falling into monetary poverty proved to be significantly lower for the second generation than the first, this decline seems to have occurred not because the conditions of access to (labour) markets and welfare have substantially improved for the second- and third-generation settlers but because their first-generation counterparts have transitioned into the retirement phase of their lives under highly unfavourable conditions. This is further supported by the lack of a significant difference in the poverty levels of the settlers from the second and third generations, remaining well above the rates recorded for their counterparts in Turkey. This group of settlers also seems to be suffering from a mismatch between their educational, occupational and income status. Hence, the observed generational trends cannot be taken at face value to suggest a substantial improvement in the predicament of settlers from younger generations.

The results are also confirmatory of Hypothesis 4, expecting poverty to be transmitted strongly among the settlers as well as the stayers due to their being largely left to their own devices in the market. The probability of transmission proved to be significant for both groups but slightly lower for the settlers. Some of the observed differences can be attributed to the welfare protection provided for families with children in destination contexts. Returnees comprise the only group who succeeded in breaking the cycle of transmission. They partly owe this to the power of migrant money and the wealth their male ancestors have accrued during their time abroad.

Before turning to address the implications of the findings for the resource-based model developed and applied in this book, a point should be made about its contribution to closing a major theoretical lacuna existing within the relevant literature. The novelty of this model stems from it situating international migration within a livelihood framework while providing the most comprehensive picture of the key causal paths between the processes of migration and migrant poverty. The model captures a wide range of micro- and macro-level factors that can potentially affect the poverty outcomes for international migrants and their descendants and explains their role in shaping their resource profiles and economic actions. The statistical analyses shed particular light upon migrant resources and some of the main factors enhancing or restricting their availability and/or capacity to deliver benefits.

Contrary to the assimilationist expectations (for example, Toledo 1969; Alba and Nee 1997), the results show that the settlers' impoverishment does not necessarily ease with the passage of *time*. Even those who spent most or the whole of their lifetime are not necessarily spared the risk of falling into monetary poverty. Compared with the returnees and stayers with the same level of education, the settlers obtain diminished monetary returns from the *formal cultural capital* they mobilise along with their labour resources. As also suggested by Obucina (2014), this may be due to a) the discriminatory practices to which they are exposed in the European labour markets, and/or b) the undervaluation of their qualifications. The most protected against the poverty risk are the returnees with university or higher degrees.

The *economic capital* resources of the settlers seem to deliver greater returns. Particularly their non-financial investments in Europe are found to possess a significant cash-generating capacity that keeps them above the poverty line. These investments tend to be made more by members of the second and third generations than the first, in line with the generational trend towards self-employment in small, low-status businesses. As compared with the settlers, the non-financial asset portfolios of the stayers and the returnees exhibit a limited capacity to generate cash, but on average, the latter two own more non-financial assets, including a house. Even if these assets do not generate rent, their use value must be indirectly contributing to poverty reduction.

The *social capital* accumulations of the settlers appear to make little difference, however. It is shown that those with more inter-ethnic ties in their friendship circles are not necessarily less impoverished in monetary terms. Following Heizmann and Böhnke (2016), these findings could be interpreted as meaning that their intra-ethnic ties are as useful as their inter-ethnic ties. However, an alternative explanation is also plausible but remains to be established empirically: the settlers might be more inclined to establish inter-ethnic ties with other minorities than the members of the majority population, and these ties may have little capacity to connect them to better places in the opportunity structure. The same may also be true for their intra-ethnic ties.

The *institutional entitlements* the settlers have acquired through becoming a destination country citizen appear to offer some protection against the risk of monetary poverty. Yet, it emerges that such legal protection does not necessarily extend to the native-born children of migrants living in destination countries like Germany.

The emerging evidence provides strong support for the findings obtained from multi-level studies by suggesting that the benefit delivery capacity of the settlers' resources is more dependent upon the context than those influences (for example, personal and household characteristics) operating at the micro level (Corrigan 2014; Bárcena-Martìn and Pérez-Moreno 2017). Larger households are found to fare badly, but this is likely to be because their adult members are left to the mercy of the labour market with little welfare protection. Destination country contexts may provide some relief from patriarchal pressures and some welfare protection for the children, but are inflicting monetary poverty upon the settlers and contributing to its perpetuation across generations, *particularly* through a) instigating diminished returns from their educational achievements, b) restricting their rights to citizenship, and/or c) denying them the generosity of the welfare states, for example, in access to pensions or other cash benefits.

Given the above, it becomes difficult not to link the root causes of the settlers' impoverishment to the systemic racism permeating most parts of the European societies and institutions, and the neo-fascist politics that keeps it alive. Unless institutional racism is completely overhauled, there is little hope for substantial improvement in the lives of 'unwanted' migrants, like those coming from Turkey, via incremental policy change.

Research limitations

Like all research, this study is not without its limitations. First of all, given the focus of the 2000 Families Survey on the labour migration from Turkey to Europe that had occurred from 1964 to 1971, the Survey is designed specifically to reflect the typical features of the guest-workers and their families through careful selection of their regional origins of migration. While the Survey captures a good proportion of the migrants from Turkey to Europe, including the post-1970 migrants who came from non-migrant families but moved subsequently, it does not speak to the entire diaspora.

Secondly, due to data restrictions, only monetary aspects of poverty could be measured, drawing on a threshold set at 60 per cent of the median equivalent disposable annual household income. The high item-response rate obtained for the income variable and random distribution of missing cases enhances the robustness of the chosen threshold. However, this study is unable to fully circumvent the potential limitations associated with income-based measures in particular, and monetary methods of poverty measurement in general. One of the problems stems from possible inaccuracies in income reporting. There may be some undetected under-reporting downwardly biasing the poverty rates but the bias is likely to be randomly distributed; hence, it is not supposed to radically change the relative picture. Another problem is to do with the arbitrariness of the choice of income threshold. Like most European studies on migrant poverty, this study followed the Eurostat (2010) guidance to set the threshold at 60 per cent of the median. The application of the 60 per cent as opposed to a 50 per cent threshold might have led to a slight upward bias in the poverty rates in countries such as Denmark with relatively more compressed disposable income distributions (Jakobsen and Pedersen 2017). However, again, the adoption of a 50 per cent threshold is highly unlikely to substantially alter the relative picture. A third problem is the narrower representation of poverty, resulting from the exclusion of its elements that cannot be attached a monetary value (for example, non-commodified access to state welfare). A multi-dimensional approach to measurement would have ensured a broader representation of poverty by allowing its monetary and non-monetary aspects to be combined; thereby, possibly yielding a very different picture.

Thirdly, again for reasons to do with data unavailability, housing costs could not be factored into the poverty measurement, causing a downward bias in the observed poverty rates. The inclusion of housing costs may have particularly worsened the rates for the settlers, as they are less likely to own a house in their country of residence than the stayers and the returnees (Eroğlu 2021).

Fourthly, due to an absence of data on household members' ages, household incomes were equivalised using the square root scale rather than the moderated OECD scale. Given the latter's tendency to create smaller economies of scale, its application might have caused a reduction in the observed poverty rates (Galloway and Aaberge 2005).

Fifthly, some of the family members covered by the Survey are likely to live in the same household and share the same income. The extent of income sharing between the respondents, however, went unmeasured. Resolution of this problem would have, for example, helped paint a clearer picture of the generational trends in monetary poverty and the extent of its transmission across family generations.

Last but not least, migrant selectivity cannot be fully eliminated due to the impracticality of a comparison of one's pre- and post-migration status. However, incorporation of the returnees into the analyses as the third comparator was of particular help in disentangling the poverty impact of international migration.

An agenda for future research

This study leaves important questions for further investigation. A central one concerns why the settlers in Europe continue to live there, despite being monetarily so impoverished. Further research might want to adopt a multi-dimensional approach to poverty measurement to illuminate this conundrum.

Questions also remain about the role of certain resource types in shaping migrant poverty. Researchers may, for example, want to demonstrate empirically the extent to which the volume and composition of migrants' and their descendants' social capital resources make a difference. This would help enlighten the question remaining about the poverty impact of their inter-and intra-ethnic friendship ties. Others may wish to focus on their economic capital resources that come in the form of financial assets (for example, savings). From an intergenerational viewpoint, further research can be conducted to investigate the type of resources being transferred from (grand)parents to (grand)children and how beneficial they are in terms of reducing poverty.

Venturing more into the behavioural realm, researchers may want to study in economic decisions and actions of migrants and their descendants and their outcomes for poverty. Given the deterioration of pay and working conditions globally, it would be worth exploring the nature and extent of in-work poverty. Another important question concerns the area of non-commodified consumption. The type and quality of the welfare services accessible to the migrants and their descendants needs examining further, as these might be key to the settlers' decision to continue living in Europe.

Relatedly, there remains a need to 'unpack' the context further. This study focussed more on the contextual differences between migrant origins and destinations than the differences within the sub-group of settlers spread across different destination contexts. Hence, the reasons for the observed variation in settlers' poverty levels warrant further investigation. Any unpacking of the context would require a detailed exploration of the conditions to which migrants are exposed within the local and national labour, asset and financial markets and welfare systems of the receiving countries and their interactions with the relevant government policies and public attitudes to migrants.

References

Abramitzky, R., Boustan, L.P. and Eriksson, K. 2013. Have the Poor Always Been Less Likely to Migrate? Evidence from Inheritance Practices during the Age of Mass Migration? *Journal of Development Economics* 102(1): 2–14.

Aguilera, M.B. and Massey, D.S. 2003. Social Capital and Wages of Mexican Migrants: New Hypotheses and Tests. *Social Forces* 82(2): 671–701.

Akgündüz, A. 2008. *Labour Migration from Turkey to Europe: 1960–1974*. Aldershot: Ashgate.

Amelina, A. and Faist, T. 2012. Denaturalising the National in Research Methodologies: Key Concepts of Transnational Studies in Migration. *Ethnic and Racial Studies* 35(10): 1707–24.

Alba, R. and Nee, V. 1997. Rethinking Assimilation Theory for a New Era of Immigration. *International Migration Review* 31(4): 826–74.

Alba, R. and Nee, V. 2003. *Remaking the American Mainstream: Assimilation and Contemporary Immigration*. Cambridge: Harvard University Press.

Alba, R.D., Jimenez, T.R. and Marrow, H.B. 2011. The Kids Are (Mostly) Alright: Second-Generation Assimilation. *Social Forces* 89(3): 763–74.

Alexander, J.T., Leibbrand, C., Massey, C. and Tolnay, S. 2017. Second-Generation Outcomes of the Great Migration. *Demography* 54(6): 2249–71.

Alkire, S. and Santos, M.E. 2010. Acute Multidimensional Poverty: A New Index for Developing Countries. Oxford Poverty & Human Development Initiative (OPHI) Working Paper No. 38, United Nations Development Programme, Human Development Report Office, Background Paper No. 2010/11. Published in Social Indicators Research Special Issue 112(2).

Alkire, S. and Santos, M.E. 2014. Measuring Acute Poverty in the Developing World: Robustness and Scope of the Multi-Dimensional Poverty Index. *World Development* 59: 251–74.

Anand, P., Jones, S., Donoghue, M. and Teitler, J. 2020. Non-Monetary Poverty and Deprivation: A Capability Approach. *Journal of European Social Policy*. https://doi.org/10.1177%2F0958928720938334

Arcagni, A., di Belgiojoso, E.B., Fattore, M. and Rimoldi, S.M.L. 2019. Multidimensional Analysis of Deprivation and Fragility Patterns of Migrants in Lombardy, Using Partially Ordered Sets and Self-Organizing Maps. *Social Indicators Research* 141(2): 551–79.

Bárcena-Martìn, E. and Pérez-Moreno, S. 2017. Immigrant-Native Gap in Poverty: A Cross-National European Perspective. *Review of Economics of the Household* 15(4): 1105–36.

Baykara-Krumme, H. 2014. Three-Generation Marriage Patterns: Insight from a Dissimilation Perspective. *Journal of Ethnic and Migration Studies* 41(8): 1324–146.

Baykara-Krumme, H. 2016 Consanguineous Marriage in Turkish Families in Turkey and in Western Europe. *International Migration Review* 50(3): 568–98.

Baykara-Krumme, H. 2017. Impact of Migration on Marriage Arrangement: A Comparison of Turkish Families in Turkey and Western Europe. *Journal of Family Issues* 38(15): 2150–77.

Baykara-Krumme, H. and Platt, L. 2018. Life Satisfaction of Migrants, Stayers and Returnees: Reaping the Fruits of Migration in Old Age? *Ageing and Society* 38(4): 721–45.

Bayrakdar, S. and Güveli, A. 2021. Understanding the Benefits of Migration: Multigenerational Transmission, Gender and Educational Outcomes of Turks in Europe. *Journal of Ethnic and Migration Studies* 47(13): 3037–58.

Bebbington, A., Hinojosa-Valencia, L., and Rojas Lizaraz, R.E. 2007. Livelihoods and Resources in Accessing the Andes: *Desencuentros* in Theory and Practice. In I. Gough and J.A. McGregory (eds) *Wellbeing in Developing Countries: From Theory to Research*, pp 176–98. Cambridge: Cambridge University Press.

Berger, J. and Mohr, J. 1975/2010. *A Seventh Man*. London: Verso.

Berti, F., D'Agostino, A., Lemmi, A. and Neri, A. 2014. Poverty and Deprivation of Migrants versus Natives in Italy. *International Journal of Social Economics* 41(8): 630–49.

Bertoli, S., Fernandez, H.M. and Ortega, F. 2013. Crossing the Border: Self-Selection, Earnings and Individual Migration Decisions. *Journal of Development Economics* 101(1): 75–91.

Blau, F.D. 1984. The Use of Transfer Payments by Immigrants. *Industrial and Labor Relations Review* 37(2): 222–39.

Blinder, S. and Markaki, Y. 2018. Europeans' Attitudes to Immigration from within and outside Europe: A Role for Perceived Welfare Impacts? Working Paper. Available at: www.reminder-project.eu/wp-content/uploads/2018/07/D10.1-Final_July-2018_with-cover.pdf. Accessed 26 June 2020.

Blume, K., Gustafsson, B., Pedersen, P.J. and Verner, M. 2007. At the Lower End of the Table: Determinants of Poverty among Immigrants to Denmark and Sweden. *Journal of Ethnic and Migration Studies* 33(3): 373–96.

Booth, C. 1891. *Life and Labour of the People of London*. Vol. 1. London: Macmillan.

Borjas, G.J. 1987. Self-Selection and the Earnings of Immigrants. *American Economic Review* 77(4): 531–53.

Borjas, G.J. and Hilton, L. 1996. Immigration and the Welfare State: Immigrant Participation in Means-Tested Entitlement Programs. *The Quarterly Journal of Economics* 111(2): 575–604.

Bourdieu, P. 1986. *Handbook of Theory and Research for the Sociology of Education*. New York: Green Wood Press.

Boyd, M. 1984. At a Disadvantage: The Occupational Attainments of Foreign Born Women in Canada. *International Migration Review* 18(4): 1091–119.

Brown, S.K. 2007. Delayed Spatial Assimilation: Multi-Generational Incorporation of the Mexican-Origin Population in Los Angeles. *City & Community* 6(3): 193–209.

Buis, M. 2015. Logistic Regression: Why We Can Often Do What We Think We Can Do Working Paper. Available at: http://maartenbuis.nl/wp/odds_ratio.pdf

Büchel, F. and Frick, J.R. 2005. Immigrants' Economic Performance across Europe: Does Immigration Policy Matter? *Population Research and Policy Review* 24(2): 175–212.

Carpio, C.C. 2017. Immigration and Economic Crisis: An Analysis of the Impact in Spain, 2007–2013. *Critical Sociology* 43(7–8): 1161–77.

Chapman, J. and Bernstein, J. 2003. Immigration and Poverty: How Are They Linked? *Monthly Labor Review* 126(4): 10–15.

Chiswick, B.R. 1978. The Effect of Americanization on the Earnings of Foreign-Born Men. *Journal of Political Economy* 86(5): 897–921.

Chiswick, B.R. 1986. Are Immigrants Favourably Selected? An Economic Analysis. In C.B. Brettell and J.F. Hollifield (eds) *Migration Theory: Talking across Disciplines*. London: Routledge, pp 61–76.

Cojanu, S.F. and Stroe, C. 2017. Poverty and Migratory Decision. Conference Proceedings Paper. 26th International Scientific Conference on Economic and Social Development – Building Resilient Society. 8–9 December, Zagreb, Croatia.

Coleman, J.S. 1988. Social Capital in the Creation of Human Capital. *American Journal of Sociology* 94(Suppl. S): 95–120.

Coniglio, N.D. and Brzozowski, J. 2018. Migration and Development at Home: Bitter or Sweet Return? Evidence from Poland. *European Urban and Regional Studies* 25(1): 85–105.

Corrigan, O. 2014. Migrant Deprivation, Conditionality of Legal Status and the Welfare State. *Journal of European Social Policy* 24(3): 223–39.

Crul, M. and Vermeulen, H. 2003. The Second Generation in Europe. *International Migration Review* 37(4): 965–86.

Crul, M., Schnell, P., Herzog-Punzenberger, B., Wilmes, M., Slootman, M. and Aparicio Gómez, R. 2012. School Careers of Second-Generation Youth in Europe: Which Education Systems Provide the Best Chances for Success? In Crul, M., Schneider, J. and Lelie, F. (eds) *The European Second Generation Compared: Does the Integration Context Matter?* Amsterdam: Amsterdam University Press.

Crul, M., Schneider, J., Keskiner, E. and Lelie, F. 2017. The Multiplier Effect: How the Accumulation of Cultural and Social Capital Explains Steep Upward Social Mobility of Children of Low-Educated Immigrants. *Ethnic and Racial Studies* 40(2): 321–38.

Crul, M., Lelie, F. and Keskiner, F. 2019. The Second and Third Generation in Rotterdam: Increasing Diversity within Diversity. In Crul, M., Scholten, P. and van Laar, P. (eds) *Coming to Terms with Superdiversity: The Case of Rotterdam*, pp 57–71.

Curtis, K.J. 2018. US Return Migration and the Decline in Southern Black Disadvantage, 1970–2000. *Social Science Quarterly* 99(3): 1214–32.

De Haas, H. 2010. Migration and Development: A Theoretical Perspective. *International Migration Review* 44(1): 227–64.

Doyal, L. and Gough, I. 1991. *A Theory of Human Need*. London: Macmillan.

Dustmann, C., Frattini, T. and Lanzara, G. 2012. Educational Achievement of Second-Generation Immigrants: An International Comparison. *Economic Policy* 27(69): 143–85.

Eichenlaub, S.C., Stewart E.T. and Alexander, J.T. 2010. Moving Out but Not Up: Economic Outcomes in the Great Migration. *American Sociological Review* 75(1): 101–25.

Emeka, A.S. 2016. Poverty and Affluence across the First Two Generations of Voluntary Migration from Africa to the United States, 1990–2012. *Sociology of Race and Ethnicity* 2(2): 162–85.

Eroğlu, Ş. 2004. What Difference Do Resources Make? A Longitudinal Study of Household Responses to Poverty in a Gecekondu Settlement in Ankara, Turkey. PhD Thesis. University of Kent: School of Social Policy, Sociology and Social Research.

Eroğlu, Ş. 2007. Developing an Index of Deprivation which Integrates Objective and Subjective Dimensions: Extending the Work of Townsend, Mack and Lansley and Halleröd. *Social Indicators Research* 80(3): 493–510.

Eroğlu, Ş. 2011. *Beyond the Resources of Poverty: Gecekondu Living in the Turkish Capital*. London: Routledge.

Eroğlu, Ş. 2013. Extending the Resource-Based Approach to Livelihoods: An Urban Application to Turkish *Gecekondu* Households. *International Journal of Urban and Regional Research* 37(2): 769–89.

Eroğlu, Ş. 2018. Trapped in Small Business? An Investigation of Three Generations of Migrants from Turkey to Western Europe. *Journal of Ethnic and Migration Studies* 44(7): 1214–32.

Eroğlu, Ş. 2020. Are Movers More Egalitarian than Stayers? An Intergenerational Perspective on Household Financial Decision-Making. *International Migration Review* 54(1): 120–46.

Eroğlu, Ş. 2021. Understanding the Consequences of Migration for Asset Accumulation: A Multi-Site and Intergenerational Perspective. *International Migration Review* 55(3): 785–811.

Eugster, B. 2018. Immigrants and Poverty, and Conditionality of Immigrants' Social Rights. *Journal of European Social Policy* 28(5): 452–70.

Eurostat. 2010. *Combating Poverty and Social Exclusion: A Statistical Portrait of the European Union 2010*. Luxembourg: Eurostat Statistical Books.

Eurostat. 2018. Euro/ECU Exchange Rates – Annual Data. Available at: https://appsso.eurostat.ec.europa.eu/nui/show.do?dataset=ert_bil_eur_a&lang=en. Accessed 26 July 2018.

Fleischmann, F. and Dronkers, J. 2010 Unemployment among Immigrants in European Labor Markets: An Analysis of Origin and Destination Effects. *Work, Employment and Society* 24(2): 337–54.

Fleury, D. 2007. *A Study of Poverty and Working Poverty among Recent Immigrants to Canada*. Final Report. Canada: Human Resources and Social Development.

Flik, R.J. and Van Praag, B.M.S. 1991. Subjective Poverty Lines Definitions. *De Economist* 139(3): 330–331.

Galloway, T.A. and Aaberge, R. 2005. Assimilation Effects on Poverty among Immigrants in Norway. *Journal of Population Economics* 18(4): 691–718.

Galloway, T.A., Gustafsson, B., Pedersen, P.J. and Österberg, T. 2009. Immigrant Child Poverty in Scandinavia: A Panel Data Study. *IZA DP*, June(no 4232): 1–40.

Gans, H.J. 1992. Second-Generation Decline: Scenarios for the Economic & Ethnic Futures of the Post-1965 American Immigrants. *Ethnic & Racial Studies* 15(2): 173–92.

Ganzeboom, H.B.G., Sözeri, E.K., Güveli, A. and Bayrakdar, S. 2016. *2000 Families: Migration Histories of Turks in Europe – Data Documentation.* Amsterdam: VU University of Amsterdam.

Gibson, J., McKenzie, D. and Stillman, S. 2013. Accounting for Selectivity and Duration Dependent Heterogeneity when Estimating the Impact of Emigration in Incomes and Poverty in Sending Areas. *Economic Development and Cultural Change* 61(2): 247–80.

Gibson, J., McKenzie, D., Rohorua, H. and Stillman, S. 2018. Long-Term Impacts of International Migration: Evidence from a Lottery. *The World Bank Economic Review* 32(1): 127–47.

Goedemé, T., Storms, B., Penne, T. and Bosch, K.V.D. 2015. The Development of a Methodology for Comparable Reference Budgets in Europe. Final report of the pilot project. Brussels: European Commission Directorate-General for Employment, Social Affairs and Inclusion.

Gordon, D. 2015. Measuring Poverty in the UK. In Dermott, E. and Main, G. (eds) *Poverty and Social Exclusion in the UK.* Bristol: Policy Press pp 17–40.

Gordon, D., Adelman, L., Ashworth, K., Bradshaw, J., Levitas, R., Middleton, S. et al 2000. *Poverty and Social Exclusion in Britain.* York: Joseph Rowntree Foundation.

Gordon, D., Eroğlu, Ş., Fahmy, E., Fifita, V., Nandy, S. and Olaya, A. 2019. *Multidimensional Child Poverty and Deprivation in Uganda: Volumes 1 & 2.* Kampala: UNICEF Uganda.

Gough, I. 2017. *Heat, Greed and Human Need. Climate Change, Capitalism and Sustainable Well-Being*. Cheltenham: Edward Elgar.

Gough, I., McGregor, J.A. and Camfield, L. 2007. Theorising Well-Being in International Development. In Gough, I. and McGregor, J.A. (eds) *Well-Being in Developing Countries* Cambridge: Cambridge University Press, pp 1–3.

Guio, A.C., Gordon, D., Najera, H. and Pomati, M. 2017. *Revising the EU Material Deprivation Variables*. Luxembourg: EUROSTAT.

Gustafsson, B. and Österberg, T. 2018. How Are Immigrant Children in Sweden Faring? Mean Income, Affluence and Poverty Since the 1980s. *Child Indicators Research* 11(1): 329–53.

Güveli, A. 2014. Are Movers More Religious than Stayers? Religiosity of European Majority, Turks in Europe and Turkey. *Review of Religious Research* 57(1): 43–62.

Güveli, A., Ganzeboom, H., Platt, L., Bernard, N., Baykara, H., Eroğlu, Ş. et al 2015. *Intergenerational Consequences of Migration: Socio-Economic, Family and Cultural Patterns of Change in Turkey and Europe*. Basingstoke: Palgrave.

Güveli, A., Ganzeboom, H., Baykara-Krumme, H., Bayrakdar, S., Eroğlu, Ş., Hamutçi, B. et al 2016. 2000 Families: Migration Histories of Turks in Europe. GESIS Archive: Leibnitz Institute for the Social Sciences. ZA5957 Data file version 2.0.0, DOI: 10.4232/1.12541.

Güveli, A., Ganzeboom, H., Baykara-Krumme, H., Platt, L., Eroğlu, Ş., Spierings, N. et al 2017. 2000 Families: Identifying the Research Potential of an Origins-of-Migration Study. *Ethnic and Racial Studies* 40(14): 2558–76.

Halleröd, B. 1994. A New Approach to the Direct Consensual Measurement of Poverty. Social Policy Research Centre Discussion Paper No. 50. Sydney: University of New South Wales.

Halleröd, B. 1995. The Truly Poor: Direct and Indirect Consensual Measurement of Poverty in Sweden. *Journal of European Social Policy* 5(2): 11–29.

Hammarstedt, M. 2001. Disposable Income Differences between Immigrants and Natives in Sweden. *International Journal of Social Welfare* 10(2): 117–26.

Hansen, J. and Wahlberg, R. 2009. Poverty and its Persistence: A Comparison of Natives and Migrants in Sweden. *Review of the Economics of the Household* 7(2): 105–32.

Hatlebakk, M. 2016. Inter-Generational Determinants of Migration Decisions: The Case of International Labour Migration from Nepal. *Oxford Development Studies* 44(1): 93–112.

Heizmann, B. and Böhnke, P. 2016. Migrant Poverty and Social Capital: The Impact of Intra- and Interethnic Contacts. *Research in Social Stratification and Mobility* 46(Part B): 73–85.

Hoaglin, D.C. and Iglewicz, B. 1987. Fine-Tuning Some Resistant Rules for Outlier Labeling. *Journal of American Statistical Association* 82(400): 1147–9.

Hooijer, G. and Picot, G. 2015. European Welfare States and Migrant Poverty: The Institutional Determinants of Disadvantage. *Comparative Political Studies* 48(14): 1879–904.

Huddleston, T., Niessen, J., Chaoimin, E.N. and White, E. 2011. *MIPEX – Migrant Integration Policy Index III*. Brussels: British Council and Migration Policy Group.

Ichou, M. 2014. Who They Were There: Immigrants' Educational Selectivity and their Children's Educational Attainment. *European Sociological Review* 30(6): 750–65.

ILO. 1976. *Employment Growth and Basic Needs: A One-World Problem*. Geneva: International Labour Organization.

IMF. 2018. World Economic Outlook Database. Available at: www.imf.org/external/pubs/ft/weo/2018/02/weodata/download.aspx. Accessed 26 July 2018.

Imran, K., Devadason, E.S. and Cheok, C.K. 2020. Foreign Remittances and Regional Poverty: Evidence from Household Data. *International Migration* 58(4): 214–30.

Jakobsen, V. and Pedersen, P.J. 2017. Poverty Risk among Older Immigrants in a Scandinavian Welfare State. *European Journal of Social Security* 19(3): 242–62.

Jensen, L. 1991. Secondary Earner Strategies and Family Poverty: Immigrant Native Differentials. *International Migration Review* 25(1): 113–39.

Kalter, F. 2011. The Second Generation in the German Labor Market: Explaining the Turkish Exception. In Alba, R. and Waters, M.C. (eds) *The Next Generation: Immigrant Youth in Comparative Perspective*. New York: New York University Press, pp 166–84.

Kasinitz, P., Mollenkopf, J.H., Waters, M.C. and Holdaway, J. 2008. *Inheriting the City: The Children of Immigrants Come of Age*. New York: Russell Sage Foundation.

Kazemipur, A. and Halli, S.S. 2001. Immigrants and 'New Poverty': The Case of Canada. *International Migration Review* 35(4): 1129–56.

Keister, L.A., Vallejo, J.A. and Smith, P.B. 2020. Investing in the Homeland: Cross-Border Investments and Immigrant Wealth in the U.S. *Journal of Ethnic and Migration Studies* 46(18): 3785–807.

Keskiner, E. and Crul, E. 2017 How to Reach the Top? Fields, Forms of Capital, and Strategies in Accessing Leadership Positions in France among Descendants of Migrants from Turkey. *Ethnic and Racial Studies* 40(2): 283–300.

Kesler, C. 2015. Welfare States and Immigrant Poverty: Germany, Sweden, and the United Kingdom in Comparative Perspective. *Acta Sociologica* 58(1): 39–61.

Kloosterman, R. 2000. Immigrant Entrepreneurship and the Institutional Context: A Theoretical Exploration. In Rath, J. (ed) *Immigrant Businesses: The Economic, Political and Social Environment*. London: Palgrave MacMillan, pp 90–106.

Kloosterman, R., Rusinovic, K. and Yeboah, D. 2016. Super-Diverse Migrants: Similar Trajectories? Ghanaian Entrepreneurship in the Netherlands Seen from a Mixed Embeddedness Perspective. *Journal of Ethnic and Migration Studies* 42(6): 913–32.

Kogan, I. 2006. Labor Markets and Economic Incorporation among Recent Immigrants in Europe. *Social Forces* 85(2): 697–721.

Konyali, A. 2017. International Opportunities on the Way up: Alternative Career Paths of Descendants of Migrants from Turkey in the Field of Professional Business Services. *Ethnic and Racial Studies* 40(2): 264–82.

Lamb, D., Banerjee, R. and Verma, A. 2021. Immigrant-Non-Immigrant Wage Differentials in Canada: A Comparison between Standard and Non-Standard Jobs. *International Migration* 59(5): 113–33.

Lee, E.S. 1966. A Theory of Migration. *Demography* 3(1): 47–57.

Lelkes, O. 2007. *Poverty Among Migrants in Europe*. Policy Brief, April. Vienna: European Centre for Social Welfare Policy and Research.

Lelkes, O. and Zólyomi, E. 2011. *Poverty and Social Exclusion of Migrants in the European Union*. Vienna: European Centre for Social Welfare Policy and Research.

Lessard-Phillips, L., Fibbi, R. and Wanner, P. 2012. Assessing the Labour Market Position and its Determinants for the Second Generation. In Crul, M., Schneider, J. and Lelie, F. (eds) *The European Second Generation Compared: Does the Integration Context Matter?* Amsterdam: Amsterdam University Press, pp 165–224.

Levels, M. and Dronkers, J. 2008. Educational Performance of Native and Immigrant Children from Various Countries of Origin. *Ethnic and Racial Studies* 31(8): 1404–25.

Lightman, N. and Gingrich, L.G. 2018. Measuring Economic Exclusion for Racialized Minorities, Immigrants and Women in Canada: Results from 2000 and 2010. *Journal of Poverty* 22(5): 398–420.

Louie, V. 2012. *Keeping the Immigrant Bargain: The Costs and Rewards of Success in America*. New York: Russell Sage Foundation.

Luthra, R.R. and Waldinger, R. 2010. Into the Mainstream? Labor Market Outcomes of Mexican Origin Workers. *International Migration Review* 44(4): 830–68.

Mack, J. and Lansley, S. 1983. *Breadline Britain: The Rise of Mass Poverty*. London: Oneworld Publications.

Mack, J. and Lansley, S. 1985. *Poor Britain*. London: George Allen & Unwin.

Marcuse, H. 1964. *One-Dimensional Man: Studies in the Ideology of Advanced Industrial Society*. Boston: Beacon Press.

Margolis, D., Miotti, L., Mouhoud, E.M. and Oudinet, J. 2013. *'To Have and Have Not': Migration, Remittances, Poverty and Inequality in Algeria*. IZA Discussion Paper 7747. Bonn: Institute for the Study of Labor.

Max-Neef, M. 1989. Human Scale Development: An Option for the Future. *Development Dialogue* 1: 5–80.

McCormick, B. and Wahba, J. 2001. Overseas Work Experience, Savings and Entrepreneurship amongst Return Migrants to LDCS. *Scottish Journal of Political Economy* 48(2): 164–78.

Mohanty, S.K., Mohapatra, S.R., Kastor, A., Singh, A.K. and Mahapatra, B. 2016. Does Employment-Related Migration Reduce Poverty in India? *Journal of International Migration and Integration* 17(3): 761–84.

Mood, C. 2010. Why We Cannot Do What We Think We Can Do and What We Can Do about It? *European Sociological Review* 26(1): 67–82.

Moser, C.O.N. 1998. The Asset Vulnerability Framework: Reassessing Urban Poverty Reduction Strategies. *World Development* 26(1): 1–19.

Muñozoz de Bustillo, R. and Anton, J.I. 2011. From Rags to Riches? Immigration and Poverty in Spain. *Population Research and Policy Review* 30(5): 661–76.

Murrugarra, E., Larrison, J. and Sasin, M. 2011. *Migration and Poverty: Toward Better Opportunities for the Poor – Directions in Development*. Washington, DC: World Bank.

Nandy, S. and Pomati, M. 2014. Applying the Consensual Method of Estimating Poverty in a Low Income African Setting. *Social Indicators Research* 124(3): 693–726.

Nauck, B. 2001. Social Capital, Intergenerational Transmission and Intercultural Contact in Immigrant Families. *Journal of Comparative Family Studies* 32(4): 465–89.

Niessen, J., Huddleston, T. and Citron, L. 2007. *MIPEX – Migrant Integration Policy Index*. Brussels: British Council and Migration Policy Group.

Nussbaum, M. 2000. *Women and Human Development: The Capabilities Approach*. Cambridge: Cambridge University Press.

Nussbaum, M. 2006. *Frontiers of Justice: Disability, Nationality and Species Membership*. Cambridge: Harvard University Press.

Obucina, O. 2014. Paths into and out of Poverty among Immigrants in Sweden. *Acta Sociologica* 57(1): 5–23.

OECD. nd. Income Distribution Database. Available at: https://stats.oecd.org/Index.aspx?DataSetCode=IDD#. Accessed 1 August 2018.

OECD. 2011. *Employment Outlook 2011*. Paris: Organisation for Economic Cooperation and Development.

OECD. 2019. *Society at a Glance: OECD Social Indicators*. Paris: Organisation for Economic Cooperation and Development.

Oropesa, R.S. and Landale, N.S. 1997. Immigrant Legacies: Ethnicity, Generation, and Children's Familial and Economic Lives. *Social Science Quarterly* 78(2): 399–416.

Pi Alperin, M. 2008. A Comparison of Multidimensional Deprivation Characteristics between Natives and Immigrants in Luxembourg. IRISS Working Paper No. 14, CEPS/INSTEAD. Differdange, Luxembourg.

Pichler, F. 2011. Success on European Labor Markets: A Cross-National Comparison of Attainment between Immigrant and Majority Populations. *International Migration Review* 45(4): 938–78.

Picot, G., Hou, F. and Coulombe, S. 2008. Poverty Dynamics among Recent Immigrants to Canada. *International Migration Review* 42(2): 393–424.

Piracha, M. and Vadean, F. 2010. Return Migration and Occupational Choice: Evidence from Albania. *World Development* 38(8): 1141–55.

Pizzorno, A. 2001. Why Pay for Petrol? Notes for a Theory of Social Capital. Paper presented at EURESCO Conference on Social Capital: International Perspectives. Exeter, 15–20 September.

Portes, A. 1995. Economic Sociology and the Sociology of Immigration: A Conceptual Overview. In Portes, A. (ed) *The Economic Sociology of Immigration: Essays on Networks, Ethnicity and Entrepreneurship*. New York: Russell Sage Foundation, pp 1–41.

Portes, A. and Zhou, M. 1993. A New Second Generation: Segmented Assimilation and its Variants. *Annals of the American Academy of Political and Social Science* 530(1): 74–96.

Portes, A. and Rumbaut, R.G. 2001. *Legacies: The Story of the Immigrant Second Generation*. Berkeley and New York: University of California Press.

Pratomo, D.S. and Jayanthakumaran, K. 2018. Returned Migrants and Remittances Alleviating Poverty: Evidence from Malang, East Java. *Economics and Sociology* 11(1): 2015–17.

Rath, J. 2000. Introduction: Immigrant Businesses and Their Economic, Politico-Institutional and Social Environment. In Rath, J. (ed) *Immigrant Businesses: The Economic, Political and Social Environment*. London: Palgrave MacMillan, pp 1–19.

Reitz, J.G., Zhang, H. and Hawkins, N. 2011. Comparisons of the Success of Racial Minority Immigrant Offspring in the United States, Canada, and Australia. *Social Science Research*, 40(4): 1051–66.

Rekers, A. and van Kempen, R. 2000. Location Matters: Ethnic Entrepreneurs and the Spatial Context. In Rath, J. (ed) *Immigrant Businesses: The Economic, Political and Social Environment*. London: Palgrave MacMillan.

Rezai, S. 2017. Self-Made Lawyers? Pathways of Socially Mobile Descendants of Migrants from Turkey in Europe. *Ethnic and Racial Studies* 40(2): 230–46.

Rowntree, B.S. 1910. *Poverty: A Study of Town Life*. London: Macmillan.

Ryan, D., Dooley, B. and Benson, C. 2008. Theoretical Perspectives on Post-Migration Adaptation and Psychological Wellbeing among Refugees: Towards a Resource-Based Model. *Journal of Refugee Studies* 21(1): 1–18.

Ryan, L., Erel, U. and Angelo, A. (eds). 2015. *Migrant Capital: Networks, Identities and Strategies*. Basingstoke: Palgrave Macmillan.

Sabates-Wheeler, R., Claudia, N. and Black, R. 2007. Migration, Legal Status and Poverty: Evidence from Return to Ghana. Working Paper T19. University of Sussex: Development Research Centre on Migration, Globalisation and Poverty.

Sabates-Wheeler, R., Sabates, R. and Castaldo, A. 2008. Tackling Poverty-Migration Linkages: Evidence from Ghana and Egypt. *Social Indicators Research* 87(2): 307–28.

Sainsbury, D. 2012. *Welfare States and Immigrant Rights: The Politics of Inclusion and Exclusion*. Oxford: Oxford University Press.

Salgado, C.D. and Ortiz, V. 2020. Mexican Americans and Wealth: Economic Status, Family and Place. *Journal of Ethnic and Migration Studies* 46(18): 3855–73.

Schneider, J. and Crul, M. 2012. Comparative Integration Theory: Participation and Belonging in Diverse European Cities. In Crul, M., Schneider, J. and Lelie, F. (eds) *The European Second Generation Compared: Does the Integration Context Matter?* Amsterdam: Amsterdam University Press.

Scruggs, L. and Allan, J. 2006. The Material Consequences of Welfare States: Benefit Generosity and Absolute Poverty in 16 OECD Countries. *Comparative Political Studies* 39(7): 880–904.

Sen, A.K. 1983. *Poverty and Famines: An Essay on Entitlement and Deprivation*. Oxford: Oxford University Press.

Sen, A.K. 1987. *The Standard of Living*. Cambridge: Cambridge University Press.

Sen, A.K. 1993. Capability and Well-Being. In Nussbaum, M. and Sen, A.K. (eds) *Quality of Life*. Oxford: Oxford University Press, pp 30–53.

Sen, A.K. 1999. *Commodities and Capabilities*. New Delhi: Oxford University Press.

Soysal, Y.N. 2012. Citizenship, Immigration, and the European Social Project: Rights and Obligations of Individuality. *British Journal of Sociology* 63(1): 1–21.

Spierings, N. 2014. Gender Equality Attitudes among Turks in Western Europe and Turkey: The Interrelated Impact of Migration and Parents' Attitudes. *Journal of Ethnic and Migration Studies* 41(5): 1–23.

Spörlein, C. and Van Tubergen, F. 2014. The Occupational Status Immigrants in Western and Non-Western Societies. *International Journal of Comparative Sociology* 55(2): 119–43.

Stark, O. and Taylor, J.E. 1989. Relative Deprivation and International Migration. *Demography* 26(1): 1–14.

Stillman, S., Gibson, J., McKenzie, D. and Rohorua, H. 2015. Miserable Migrants? Natural Experiment Evidence on International Migration and Objective and Subjective Well-Being. *World Development* 65(1): 79–93.

Streeton, P., Burki, S.J., Haq, M., Hicks, N. and Stewart, F. 1981. *First Things First: Meeting Basic Needs in Developing Countries.* London: Oxford University Press.

Sullivan, D.H. and Ziegert, A.L. 2008. Hispanic Immigrant Poverty: Does Ethnic Origin Matter? *Population Research and Policy Review* 27(6): 667–87.

Swift, J. 1989. Why Are Rural People Vulnerable to Famine? *IDS Bulletin* 20(1): 8–15.

Telles, E.E. and Ortiz, V. 2008. *Generations of Exclusion: Mexican Americans, Assimilation, and Race.* New York: Russell Sage Foundation.

Thomas, K.J. 2011. Familial Influences on Poverty among Young Children in Black Immigrant, US-Born Black and Nonblack Immigrant Families. *Demography* 48(2): 437–60.

Tienda, M. and Jensen, L. 1986. Immigration and Social Program Participation: Dispelling the Myth of Dependency. *Social Science Research* 15(4): 327–400.

Todaro, M.P. 1969. A Model for Labor Migration and Urban Unemployment in Less Developed Countries. *American Economic Review* 59(1): 138–48.

Townsend, P. 1979. *Poverty in the United Kingdom: A Survey of Household Resources and Standards of Living.* Berkeley and Los Angeles: University of California.

UNDP. 1990. *Human Development Report 1990.* Oxford: Oxford University Press.

UNDP. 2010. *Human Development Report 2010.* New York: United Nations Development Programme.

UNSTATS. 2005. *Handbook on Poverty Statistics: Concepts, Methods and Policy Use.* New York: United Nations Statistics Division.

Vacaflores, D.E. 2018. Are Remittances Helping Lower Poverty and Inequality Levels in Latin America? *Quarterly Review of Economics and Finance* 68(C): 254–65.

Van Hook, J., Brown, S. and Kwenda, M.N. 2004. A Decomposition of Trends in Poverty among Children of Immigrants. *Demography* 41(4): 649–70.

Van Tubergen, F. 2006. Occupational Status of Immigrants in Cross-National Perspective: A Multilevel Analysis of 17 Western Societies. In Parsons, C.A. and Smeeding, T.M. (eds) *Immigration and the Transformation of Europe*. Cambridge: Cambridge University Press, pp 147–71.

Van Tubergen, F., Flap, H. and Mass, I. 2004. The Economic Incorporation of Immigrants in 18 Western Societies: Origin, Destination, and Community Effects. *American Sociological Review* 69(5): 704–27.

Veit-Wilson, J.H. 1986. Paradigms of Poverty: A Rehabilitation of B.S. Rowntree. *Journal of Social Policy* 15(1): 69–99.

Villarreal, A. and Tamborini, C. 2018. Immigrants' Economic Assimilation: Evidence from Longitudinal Earnings Records. *American Sociological Review* 83(4): 686–715.

Wagle, U.R. and Devkota, S. 2018. The Impact of Foreign Remittances on Poverty in Nepal: A Panel Study of Household Survey Data, 1996–2011. *World Development* 110(October): 38–50.

Whelan, C.T. and Maître, B. 2007. Measuring Material Deprivation with EU-SILC: Lessons from the Irish Survey. *European Societies* 9(2): 147–73.

Wisor, S. 2012. *Measuring Global Poverty: Towards a Pro-Poor Approach*. London: Palgrave Macmillan.

Wong, R., Palloni, A. and Soldo, B.J. 2007. Wealth in Middle and Old Age in Mexico: The Role of International Migration. *International Migration Review* 41(1): 127–51.

World Bank. No Date. Understanding Poverty. Available at: www.worldbank.org/en/topic/poverty. Accessed 2 October 2021.

Young, M.E.D., Leon-Perez, G., Wells, C.R. and Wallace, S.P. 2018. More Inclusive States, Less Poverty Among Immigrants? An Examination of Poverty, Citizenship Stratification, and State Immigrant Policies. *Population Research and Policy Review* 37(2): 205–28.

Zuccotti, C., Ganzeboom, H. and Güveli, A. 2017. Has Migration Been Beneficial for Migrants and their Children? Comparing Social Mobility of Turks in Western Europe, Turks in Turkey and Western European Natives. *International Migration Review* 51(1): 97–126.

Index

References to figures appear in *italic* type; those in **bold** type refer to tables. References to footnotes show both the page number and the note number (51n1).

Y

Z